A
Slice
of
the Pie

A Slice of the Pie

How to Build a Big Little Business

NICK SARILLO

Portfolio / Penguin

PORTFOLIO / PENGUIN
Published by the Penguin Group
Penguin Group (USA) Inc., 375 Hudson Street, New York, New York 10014, U.S.A.
Penguin Group (Canada), 90 Eglinton Avenue East, Suite 700, Toronto, Ontario, Canada
M4P 2Y3 (a division of Pearson Penguin Canada Inc.)
Penguin Books Ltd, 80 Strand, London WC2R 0RL, England
Penguin Ireland, 25 St. Stephen's Green, Dublin 2, Ireland (a division of Penguin Books Ltd)
Penguin Books Australia Ltd, 250 Camberwell Road, Camberwell, Victoria 3124, Australia
(a division of Pearson Australia Group Pty Ltd)
Penguin Books India Pvt Ltd, 11 Community Centre, Panchsheel Park,
New Delhi – 110 017, India
Penguin Group (NZ), 67 Apollo Drive, Rosedale, Auckland 0632, New Zealand
(a division of Pearson New Zealand Ltd)
Penguin Books (South Africa) (Pty) Ltd, 24 Sturdee Avenue, Rosebank, Johannesburg 2196,
South Africa

Penguin Books Ltd, Registered Offices: 80 Strand, London WC2R 0RL, England

First published in 2012 by Portfolio / Penguin, a member of Penguin Group (USA) Inc.

1   3   5   7   9   10   8   6   4   2

Photographs by Ben Rodig
Other illustrations by the author
"Safe Space" © 1997, 2008, 2011 Miick & Associates. All rights reserved.

LIBRARY OF CONGRESS CATALOGING-IN-PUBLICATION DATA
Sarillo, Nick.
A slice of the pie : how to build a big little business / Nick Sarillo.
p. cm.
Includes index.
ISBN 978-1-59184-458-7
1. New business enterprises.   2. Industrial management.   3. Employees—Training of.
4. Success in business.   I. Title.
HD62.5.S2777 2012
658.02'2—dc23   2012019321

Printed in the United States of America
Designed by Spring Hoteling

ALWAYS LEARNING   PEARSON

AUTHOR'S NOTE

To protect the privacy of the individuals involved, I have changed some names and identifying characteristics.

I dedicate this book to my reason for being, the light of my life every day—my children, **Michelle**, **Nicholas**, and **Danny**. They know I love them and that I am extremely grateful for and proud of them and the people they have turned out to be.

CONTENTS

FOREWORD

The Origins of Trust-and-Track

I first got wind of Nick's Pizza & Pub from a friend of mine, Will Phillips. Will shares my interest in companies that defy conventional wisdom about what a business can be and do, so when he heard about a pizza restaurant near Chicago where customers occasionally left tips of $500 or even $1,000, he told me about it. "Who does that?" he asked. "It's the kind of donation someone might make to a church or a charity, not to a server at a local pizza place." I agreed that something unusual must be happening at this restaurant and decided to check it out for myself.

In October 2008, Will and I headed out to Crystal Lake, Illinois, to attend an all-day seminar at Nick's Pizza & Pub. There we met Nick Sarillo, the former construction worker who had started the restaurant despite lacking any experience in the food industry. Nick and members of his team explained the management system they'd developed, as well as the philosophy behind it, and gave us a tour of the premises. I couldn't help but be impressed. Clearly, they had cracked some kind of motivational code and created a culture that, among other things, was able to turn high school kids into dream employees—smart, dedicated, resourceful, hardworking, eager to learn, willing to go out of their way to make customers happy. Nick told us how parents would come up to him and say, "I don't know what you've done to my kid, but whatever it is, please keep doing it." The results were a staff that provided great service and its concomitants: intense customer loyalty and an extraordinarily close bond with the surrounding community.

Nick was obviously proud of his restaurants, and deservedly so. He struck me as a kind of organizational miner who had hit a rich source of management gold, and his discovery so inspired him that he could hardly wait to share his bounty with the rest of the world. He'd already opened another restaurant in nearby Elgin. He was working on his third in the Portage Park neighborhood of Chicago. I came away determined to write about Nick's at the earliest opportunity, which turned out to be almost exactly one year later.

Much had changed by the time I had returned to Crystal Lake in October 2009. The Great Recession had taken a toll. The deal to open a Chicago restaurant had collapsed, and the Elgin restaurant was struggling. But Nick had lost none of his enthusiasm for, and faith in, his approach to management. Furthermore, he had learned some critical lessons in that period, and had become a wiser leader as a result.

Nick had gotten his first inkling of what those lessons might be when he refocused his attention on the Crystal Lake and Elgin restaurants after scrapping the plan to expand into Chicago proper. In gearing up for growth, he had hired new general managers for each of those restaurants, in addition to the person whom he'd tagged to eventually run the Chicago place. All three came out of large, established restaurant chains. Nick had assumed he needed people with considerable restaurant experience if he was going to grow the business as aggressively as he'd hoped. So he was surprised at some of the problems that cropped up in his absence—in particular, the difficulty the new managers seemed to have in keeping the food and beverage costs under control.

As he began to investigate, he soon realized that the problems went deeper than he'd imagined. He discovered, for example, that the manager at Elgin—we'll call him "John"—wasn't handling the beverage- and food-buying the way he'd been trained. That was why the restaurant's costs were out of control. Nick questioned him to make sure he knew how the systems were supposed to work, and he appeared to understand, but week after week the purchases did not line up with the inventory counts. When Nick did it himself, the numbers worked out fine. So why could he do it and John couldn't?

At the same time, Nick was hearing about cultural problems at Crystal Lake. The general manager there—let's call him "Jamal"—hadn't been walking the talk. "People told me he'd promise to fix something and then wouldn't do it," Nick said. "Or he'd ask team members to use our values language and then didn't use it himself. You can't do that with today's generation. They track the leader more than any previous generation in terms of what we ask people to do. If you don't follow through, you lose them."

The discovery of his managers' shortcomings only raised more questions for Nick. How had he missed the problems for so long? Were there warning signs he'd overlooked? If he couldn't count on people with the kinds of qualifications John and Jamal had, where was he going to find the leaders he'd eventually need to grow the business?

In any case, he concluded that he'd made a serious mistake in hiring senior managers from traditionally run restaurant chains. "They were trained in command-and-control, and they couldn't let go of old habits," Nick told me. "They thought it was their responsibility to tell people what to do. That's not our culture. When you manage that way, people see it, and they start waiting for you to tell them what to do. You wind up with too much on your plate, and things fall through the cracks.

"That's basically the reason they weren't hitting their food and beverage numbers. They had other people put in the costs. When the numbers came out wrong, they didn't go deeper to find out why. They weren't interested. They didn't think it was their job. So they didn't share the why with the team members. When you know the why, it's really easy to figure out what to do, but sharing that kind of information wasn't how they'd learned to manage."

But Nick realized that stubborn old habits weren't the whole story. "Command-and-control is easier in some ways, but it carries a big risk," he says. "You always have to be afraid of people finding out your imperfections, because then they'll see through you, and you won't have power over them. If your self-esteem is based on having that position of power, transparency is dangerous. But in our culture, transparency is essential. One of our values is to communicate openly, clearly, and honestly. You can't do that if you're unwilling to be transparent. Team members call me out on my imperfections, and I love it. It's not a threat if you have a culture based on trust. In fact, it proves that the trust is there."

I found all this quite fascinating. Nick's experience offered new insight into why command-and-control is often a less efficient and less effective way to run a company than . . . than . . . than what? It occurred to me that we didn't have a name for the alternatives to command-and-control, although people had been experimenting with alternatives for decades, going back at least to the Scanlon Plans of the 1930s and maybe even earlier. The perceived need for a better way of managing had been the impetus behind Theory Y, employee engagement, total quality management, lean management, team-based management, open-book management, and dozens of other similar approaches. They were all, in their own way, attempts to fashion an alternative to command-and-control aimed at harnessing the full creative and productive capacity of employees, and yet we didn't have a word or phrase to describe what tied them together.

The absence of such a term was significant, I realized. It is extremely difficult to discuss a phenomenon, a trend, or a concept that doesn't have a name. Without the language to talk about something, its very existence is tenuous at best. That said, all names are not equal. A good name captures the essence of whatever is being characterized. From that perspective, command-and-control was a very good name, indeed. I could see that it would be helpful to have an equally descriptive term for Nick's alternative to command-and-control. But what should it be?

I was still pondering that question when I met Jenny Petersen, the new Operating Partner of the Nick's Pizza & Pub in Elgin, who was twenty-four years old at the time. She'd started as a host in the Crystal Lake restaurant when she was sixteen, while she was in high school. In 2005 she'd left to attend the University of Iowa. After graduating with a degree in psychology, she'd looked for a job in health care, in vain. Finally, at her mother's suggestion, she'd stopped by Nick's and learned that the company was looking for a manager. She'd applied and was hired to work at Elgin.

One of her early assignments had been to get on top of the beverage costs. She'd begun doing inventories every Wednesday. It was a job she enjoyed. "Our beverage cost is supposed to be 23.1 percent of sales or a little under," she told me. "If the number is off, there has to be an explanation. Maybe we counted wrong. Maybe an order wasn't entered properly. Maybe we've had more large parties than usual. There's got to be a reason. I like finding out what it is."

It had taken her barely a month to master the process, and she'd consistently hit the numbers thereafter. I couldn't help wondering why she'd been able to do what had constantly eluded her older and more experienced predecessor. "She just kept digging," said Debbie Buttice, a server at Elgin who worked with Petersen on the inventory counts. "Before, nobody was investigating. If we missed one week, the attitude was, 'Maybe it will be better next week.' There was no sense of urgency."

That, in a nutshell, was the difference between a command-and-control culture and one based on the principles that Nick believed in. The contrast could not have been more stark. "I kept explaining to [John, the old manager] how the system was supposed to work," Nick said. "I thought that maybe it was too complex. But then Jenny got it right away. That made me realize that our systems are simple enough. Now I know that, when I find myself repeating what I've already taught, it should be a red flag that something else is getting in the way of understanding."

But Nick also recognized that he'd missed a lot of other red flags along the way, which suggested that his system needed something else to work as well as it should. "The big lesson is accountability," he said. "Leaders must follow through and do what they said they'd do. I wasn't holding those managers accountable for their results and their behaviors. But along with that, I need to be clear about what I want and to state it clearly. The clearer I am, the less I have to hold people accountable. And I can't be optimistic for people. Results are results. I have to be real about how people are doing. You know, when you have a culture like this, there's a tendency to think you just have to be nice. I went to hear the Dalai Lama, who spoke about the difference between being nice and being kind. I have to be kind, not nice. Being nice doesn't support anything. Being kind means being real."

So I realized that the alternative to command-and-control—whatever form it may take—had two components. One of them clearly had to do with creating a climate of trust, which is always a two-way street. For the system to work, it's critical that employees trust management to tell the truth and to keep its word, and that management trusts employees to do the right thing for the company. But trust alone is not enough. There is also an accountability aspect. I wondered, What term would encompass both elements?

In retrospect, the answer was obvious, though I admit I needed help to see it. One friend suggested that the right phrase was "delegate-and-trust." I ran that by another friend who said, "I call that 'trust-and-hope.' I tried it and it cost me $20 million." Okay, I thought, what about Ronald Reagan's term—"trust, but verify"? That formulation encapsulated both elements, but when I suggested it to two other friends—Paul Spiegelman, founder and CEO of The Beryl Companies, and Ping Fu, cofounder and CEO of Geomagic—they thought it sounded a bit harsh, as if employees couldn't really be trusted and needed to be constantly checked up on. We kicked around various other ideas until someone—I don't remember who—suggested "trust-and-track." All three of us knew immediately that we'd found it. Alternatives to command-and-control were all based on trust-and-track. It even had the right alliteration!

As you will see in the pages that follow, Nick and his colleagues have put together a particularly inspiring version of trust-and-track management. In the process, they have made significant contributions to our understanding of how such systems differ from traditional command-and-control and why they work so well. His restaurants are living proof of trust-and-track's effectiveness in bringing out the best in people—not just employees, but managers, customers, and members of the communities that a business serves.

But Nick's story also highlights a fundamental truth: namely, that numbers run businesses. It's a truth I learned from another friend of mine, Norm Brodsky, who—like Nick—learned it the hard way. Whatever the advantages of trust-and-track, you simply won't have the opportunity to practice it, or any other form of management, if you don't understand and pay close attention to what the numbers are trying to tell you. In the beginning, Norm didn't, and his first company wound up in Chapter 11 as a result. Nick narrowly avoided that fate, thanks to the support he received from the community he had been serving for many years. While Nick is not out of the woods as of this writing, he has accomplished what many would have considered impossible—making an ally out of the bank to which he owed more money than he could pay back. However that situation plays out, he can take heart from what happened to Norm, who learned the lessons and went on to build a wildly successful, and profitable, small giant. Armed with trust-and-track, Nick is well on his way to doing the same. The lessons in this wonderful book show us all how to follow in their footsteps.

—Bo Burlingham, author of *Small Giants* and
editor-at-large of *Inc.* magazine

Preface
The E-mail

Every small business faces its share of turmoil, and many don't make it. In the fall of 2011, I was convinced mine was going to be one of those businesses—another local pizza restaurant that succumbed to the pressures of a bad economy. Luckily, I was wrong.

Like millions of Americans, I had gotten myself into a hole by borrowing too much when times were good, banking on the strength of the real estate market. In 2005 I had spent $5 million building a second restaurant location in a suburban Chicago town near my very successful first location. The town was undergoing rapid development, and we anticipated that tens of thousands of new residents would need a place to take their families for a fun dinner. We even thought we'd open a third location in downtown Chicago. Then the recession of 2007 hit, and the housing market collapsed. All those new tract homes didn't get built, which meant I was sitting on a restaurant whose revenues were half of what we had anticipated. Good luck trying to make a profit while also making those hefty mortgage payments each month.

Although our sales at the second location went up and down, the overall drag of excessive overhead persisted. By 2011 our business overall at both restaurants was in the red, and by the middle of September, it became apparent we wouldn't be able to make our payroll in a couple of weeks. I had already cut expenses to the bone and renegotiated terms with our vendors. I had met with our bankers and even consulted with a marketing guru and other experts to see what else I could do to build our business. Now I thought about two other options of last resort: finding new investors and trying to obtain a short-term loan, which would come with high interest. Over a period of a few days, I spoke to potential investors and came away empty-handed. I also truly didn't see how a Band-Aid solution like a high-interest loan would make any sense. In a few months, I'd be back in the same horrible position.

On September 23, our in-house accountant and I reviewed our latest cash-flow projections. The numbers looked bad, but being a stubborn optimist by nature, I blocked out any negative feelings and resolved to keep at it for the rest of the day. The next morning, a Saturday, it finally hit me. We were facing a $128,000 deficit by the first week of October. This was it. I was out of options. Barring a miracle, I would have to declare bankruptcy and give up the business I had worked so hard to build for the past sixteen years. I felt heartbroken at the thought of what this would mean for our team members who showed up for work every day, not to mention for the family and friends who had supported me and who depended on me financially. I literally put my head in my hands and cried. "Oh, well," I thought, "if this is it, I guess I did my best." An overwhelming sense of surrender and acceptance washed over me.

I thought about what I would need to do next. I knew I had a responsibility to let my community of team members, guests, and vendors know what was happening, so I turned on my computer, pulled up a blank document, and began to draft an e-mail. "I have never understood why owners or management of a failing company usually don't give others close to the company—especially customers—fair warning about what is going on. . . . I have always said I would never do that to the people I truly care about and owe my life to." I went on to announce that thanks to mismanagement on my part, we would soon be forced to close, and I asked people to come in one last time to help us out. Who knows, I thought, if enough of them did, maybe we could beat the overwhelming odds and pull through. If not, then I'd have to live with the consequences.

The next day felt downright surreal. Imagining for the first time what life would be like without my company to run, I passed the e-mail by a few trusted friends, who encouraged me to go with my gut and send it. My public relations firm, to which I'd placed an emergency call, thought it was a terrible idea. Rather than address a seemingly insoluble crisis, I would only pile on a new publicity crisis that would affect morale among my team and vendors. At their request, I let the e-mail sit another night and waited to see if they could come up with any better ideas. Was I really ready to own up to my own failures so publicly and ask for help? Was I ready to risk suffering the lambasting I anticipated from the media and others? For so many years, I had run my company around a higher purpose in hopes of building strong, meaningful relationships with everyone in our community. Time and again, people had questioned this approach, thinking it too idealistic for an ordinary business like a pizza restaurant, but still I had pressed on. Now, in this moment of crisis, how deep had that relationship building gone? How far would these relationships carry me? Would people in our community care enough to come to my aid?

The next day, I decided I needed to find out. I would stick with my values and communicate what was in my heart, come what may. I took a deep breath, closed my eyes, and with a trembling finger, pressed send.

INTRODUCTION
Culture for the Rest of Us

When I first opened a pizza restaurant in the mid-1990s, people assumed it would fail. Not only is the restaurant industry notoriously difficult for start-ups, but I had never run a restaurant and was not a particularly great pizza maker. I had not finished college, I had never taken a business class (I'd never even read a business book, let alone thought about writing one), and I was making a fine living with my own carpentry business. Why would I want to risk everything for a pipe dream?

Today, having pulled through the crisis that almost sank us, my two-location restaurant, Nick's Pizza & Pub, is alive and well. We are among the top ten busiest independent pizza chains in the United States, as measured in per-unit sales. Our margins are often twice those of the average pizza joint, while employee turnover is less than 20% of the industry average. Each of our two 350-seat restaurants in suburban Chicago brings in approximately $3.5 million a year. We've been written up in *Newsweek* and in *Inc.* magazine for our innovative business practices. Best of all, our company is beloved in our community; we've won award after award and are sustaining thousands of enthusiastic fans on Facebook.

What's our secret? How did a blue-collar, born-and-bred-Midwestern boy like me take one of the most ubiquitous business ideas in America—the local pizza chain—and turn it into something extraordinary? How did we become a big little business, what *Inc.* magazine editor Bo Burlingham calls a "small giant"? It's not our pizza, and I know this because my father had used the exact recipe years earlier in his own small pizza shop, with very different results. In fact, my uncle, who bought my father's business, continues to use the same recipe, again with different results. It's not our advertising, since we don't do any. It's not the physical locations of our restaurants; others nearby aren't nearly as busy, and we're almost forty minutes outside of Chicago. Finally, as easy as it would be for me, as founder and CEO, to take all the credit, I can tell you with all honesty that it isn't me.

Our secret sauce (pardon the pun) can be summed up in one word: *culture*. At Nick's, we organize our entire business around delivering a unique and meaningful experience for our people, our customers, and our community at large. And it pays off—at moments of crisis and at all times.

We hear a lot these days about how vital culture is to organizational success. Countless articles and books detail the efforts of innovative companies like Apple, Whole Foods, Starbucks, and Southwest Airlines to create nurturing environments in which work is meaningful and employees and customers thrive. Yet such examples seem hard to emulate in places (like pizza restaurants) where turnover is generally high, a college degree is not required, and most employees consider their jobs a way to make money—not a stepping-stone to an outstanding career.

In your average small business, culture doesn't seem to

matter too much. Owners, entrepreneurs, or managers focus on more "practical" matters, like tracking the competition, keeping employees in line, and taking actions to increase volume and reduce costs. Managers hire warm bodies to fill positions; they launch new employees into jobs with scarcely any training or performance feedback, and offer them few chances to make decisions and take responsibility. As a result, employees seldom derive a sense of higher meaning from their work, nor do they feel they are growing very much as people. They perform poorly and turn over often, creating a need to hire still more warm bodies. Any improvements to the business originate with the owners, who in turn come to expect that their teams don't care very much about company success. The cycle repeats, and the result is mediocrity as well as the familiar belief that "this is just the way it is."

What we've proven at Nick's is that you don't need to be a large, sexy, headline-grabbing company to have a great culture. You can reap all the benefits of a world-class culture—including more enthusiastic teams, lower attrition, more innovation, better customer service, more sustainability, and, ultimately, better financial performance—by disciplining yourself and your organization to work the company's culture into every decision you make and every action you take.

Culture is a collection of attitudes, beliefs, and behaviors that yield a shared system of meaning. It exists in all of our organizations, whether we recognize it or not, and if we ignore it, we don't have any control over how it evolves. To achieve high performance, we can and must *shape* culture—through systems, policies, and practices, through our own behavior and that of our teammates. Culture needs to be the primary thing we do, the focal point of our professional efforts, not just something we tinker with halfheartedly when everything else is working okay.

It may be counterintuitive, but I know that unique, inspiring, transformative cultures are latent within even the smallest, most ordinary, most commoditized, and most poorly performing of organizations. Even the humble pizza parlor or corner grocery has the potential to change the world. What's required is for leaders to define the desired culture and work single-mindedly to nurture it and make it real.

THE CRAZY STUFF THAT HAPPENS WHEN YOU FALL OFF A LADDER

My life as a pizza entrepreneur began one day in the fall of 1993 when I fell off a ladder at a construction site. I was working as a carpenter, building a tract home in partnership with my brother. I might have broken a hip or a leg except that, lucky for me, I slowed my fall by catching my elbow on several metal rungs of the ladder on the way down. As I nursed my badly chipped elbow over the next few weeks, I got to thinking about my life and my career. I had gotten into building homes because I loved providing quality and expert craftsmanship, but unfortunately, the market had shifted and consumers wanted cheaper, low-end houses. Guys like me couldn't make a living unless we cut corners and put out a product we didn't believe in. I was still doing well financially, but little by little I had lost my passion for the job.

Around that time I took my three young kids, Michelle, Nicholas, and Danny, out for dinner in the town of Crystal Lake, where I was living at the time. I'd been hoping for a relaxing, pleasant dinner—something to take my mind off the inner crisis I was having—but I was disappointed. Although billed as a family restaurant, the place I chose was pretty stiff and not geared to the needs of kids; the unfriendly staff even seemed impatient with the restless behavior of Danny, my youngest. I thought to myself, "Why isn't there a restaurant in this area where families can go to just relax and have fun in a safe, comfortable, welcoming environment?" Over the weeks that followed, as I reflected further on my dissatisfaction with building houses, I thought, "Why don't *I* build a restaurant like that?"

There were many reasons, as people from my neighborhood didn't hesitate to point out. Even my own father told me I was nuts (to put it mildly).

But being called nuts—especially by Dad—only fired my determination. I had played football and was a wrestler in high school, and I was used to psyching myself up to face a challenge. Beyond that, I had seen firsthand what my dad's humble business had done for his community. People came into his place with their families and constantly told him how much they enjoyed dining there and relaxing with the ones they loved. I didn't want to just make a living; like many entrepreneurs, I wanted to devote my life to something bigger. I wouldn't have been able to express it then, but I wanted the sense of well-being that comes when you work with a higher purpose in mind, and I strongly believed in the higher purpose I'd happened on: supporting families and my community by offering them a place to relax and have fun.

In May 1995, I opened Nick's Pizza & Pub in Crystal Lake. I designed and built the place myself, with the help of family and friends. Opening the place took longer than anticipated, and I almost ran out of money, but somehow we pulled it off—and guess what? The naysayers were wrong. We didn't close that first year. Nor the year after that. Nor the year after that. We were busy from day one, and revenues and guest counts only increased from there.

We've had our struggles, some of which I'll detail in this book, but from the beginning there was something different about Nick's, something special. Customers felt it the moment they walked in the door, and they still feel it today. It was our dedication to serving families, team members, and the community with the utmost enthusiasm, warmth, and respect, a dedication that reflected my own personal passion as well as the heart and soul, and the talent and intellect, of our team members. As I'll explain in this book, this dedication has given rise to our unique culture and been sustained by it in turn. The two are so close as to be one and the same.

We've taken extreme care, first intuitively and then consciously and methodically, to design, build, and nourish that culture. Growth has challenged us, but we haven't faltered, and we've managed to understand our culture better, refine it, and develop internal processes and systems to render it scalable. Thanks to business consultants, a determined management team, inspiring books I've read, and intensive personal coaching I've received, we've engineered and honed everything—from our marketing to our hiring to our meetings to our financial systems—in order to help make our higher commitment to family and community deeper and more pronounced. We've also trained ourselves as individuals to become increasingly mindful of how we serve families and community with every action we take, both on and off the job.

As a result, daily life at our organization has become richer, more meaningful, and more fun for everyone. Our workforce has become more committed and more talented. Our customers have become more numerous and happier. Our financial results have improved, and we've survived the tough times every business goes through. In sum, taking control of culture rather than letting it just happen—constructing the culture we *wanted* rather than plodding on with the culture we had—has allowed us to do great things for all our stakeholders. As our guests say all the time, they don't quite know why, but our pizza "just tastes better."

JENNY

I've already mentioned benefits that come with a great culture—increased worker satisfaction, reduced attrition, and higher productivity. But what do these things really mean? To give you a nuts-and-bolts sense of the way high-performance culture can lead to real results for an everyday, blue-collar, commodity business like mine, and to preview things we do to support our culture, I'd like to introduce you to Jenny, one of our star team members.

Jenny is twenty-six years old and of medium height and build. When customers first meet her, the first thing they notice is her quirkiness. She's got her fair share of piercings and tattoos, a stripe of purple or tan in her hair, and thick black eyeliner that definitely makes a statement (though what kind of statement I'm not so sure). Based on her appearance alone, Jenny is not the kind of person most companies break down the doors to hire, and she is certainly not the kind of person most owners trust to run a $3.5-million chunk of business.

Yet that's precisely what Jenny does for us. Because the

second thing people notice about Jenny is her high-energy personality. She exudes happiness, health, and positive energy, and customers love her. As a result she not only succeeds at her job; she excels!

Jenny isn't a professionally trained manager. She hasn't worked at Google or Whole Foods, she doesn't have an MBA, and she didn't come to us from outside. She started at Nick's in 2003 when she was only sixteen, working part-time after school and on weekends to earn extra money. Thanks to our extensive, meticulously crafted hiring process, which includes multiple interviews and a personality test, we were able to identify her from among a large pool of applicants as someone whose personality and approach to life matched our culture of dedicated service to families and community. We specifically sought her out because we liked her independent thinking, her unwillingness to sacrifice her identity to please others, and her eagerness to share her spirit and unique perspective. In short, we thought she possessed a strong, internal sense of purpose, one that matched our own organizational purpose pretty well.

In Jenny's first position, as a host, she showed herself to be far more focused than the typical teenager, not as prone to the usual high school gossip and drama. Within months, she had taken advantage of our unusual training program, again meticulously crafted to support our culture of service, to learn basic skills in a number of roles, from dining room host to pizza maker to carry-out host, and she had also become well versed in a set of powerful leadership tools that would allow her to push our organizational purpose ever further. She continued to distinguish herself as an eager, self-motivated learner during her junior and senior years in high school, and she even helped me write one portion of our training manual for a new position we'd created called Host Coordinator.

In 2005 Jenny went off to the University of Iowa and earned a degree in psychology, working part-time at a jeweler in Iowa City. In most businesses like mine, where young employees come and go, that would have been the last an employer would have seen or heard of someone like Jenny, apart from perhaps the occasional visit or stint of summertime work. But Jenny had other ideas. After graduation in 2008, she worked at the jeweler, rising within a year to become a manager. But rather than continue in that job, she decided to return to Nick's in hopes of becoming an Operating Partner (a position that at other restaurants is commonly called General Manager). According to Jenny, our unique culture figured decisively in her decision. "I saw for myself that there was no place quite like Nick's. I loved the impact we had on the families that came in and on the community as a whole. I've always wanted to have an impact on peoples' lives, and I felt Nick's gave me that chance."

When we hired Jenny back, we didn't guarantee we'd make her Operating Partner; I had no idea whether she'd make the grade. But Jenny worked hard, and within a year of returning in 2009, she had achieved her goal. Today she bears responsibility for the full profit-and-loss statement, and she dissects the numbers better than anyone I've seen, even without a degree in accounting or finance. Diligent in her follow-through, she outperforms almost everyone in our company, contributing more profit to the bottom line than even the experienced industry professional I'd brought in to help oversee our operations. She manages ninety-five team members, some of them twice her age. Always inspired and inspiring when she comes to work, she coaches our people, in the moment, about how to serve families better, pays attention to how she coaches, models our purpose, talks about it, and recognizes it in others. In short, she does everything we'll identify in this book as pivotal for building a high-performance culture.

As great as Jenny's story is, retention, job satisfaction, and productivity hardly convey how high-performance culture can transform the typical workplace. At Nick's, we don't just retain people and get them to produce more—we retain *superior* people who go on to make careers with us and do outstanding things. Over time, a positive dynamic takes root that benefits every part of the business. Because of team members like Jenny, people love eating at our restaurants, and our reputation spreads among the community, leading more people like Jenny to apply to work for us. Once they come onboard, they too are happy. They're flourishing. They're learning and expanding. They're motivated to work on our behalf because they care deeply about our success, above and beyond the paycheck they receive. They identify personally with the organization. They *want* to identify personally with us, because they perceive us as different.

At Nick's we've created a cult in the best sense of the word, but we've also created a sustainable company that will endure long after I'm gone. That's because outstanding team members like Jenny are constantly pushing our business further, in ways I never could have imagined and without me standing over them to do it. Not bad for a local pizza restaurant you've probably never heard of.

MOBILIZING AROUND A HIGHER PURPOSE

Most businesses focus on shaping what their customers or the larger marketplace or their suppliers think of them. They concern

themselves with crafting a brand in the eyes of outsiders so that
people will buy what they're trying to sell. At Nick's, we don't
emphasize our external brand. We proceed from the inside out,
thinking about why we're here and the purpose we're trying to
serve. Our managers' main job is to discipline the organization to
align itself ever more closely to our purpose of creating a fun family environment; our reason for being is in the present tense, and
we call it the Nick's Experience. Quite naturally, even effortlessly,
and without expenditure of added capital, our company winds up
also having the best possible brand. It's no accident that we spend
zero dollars each year on advertising. Marketing for us is purely an
extension of our culture.

The following chapters present governing principles not
merely for organizing a high-performance culture, but also for
doing so around a higher purpose that is unique to you. These
principles cover many areas of running a company, including
recruiting, training, financial management, performance measurements, internal communications, marketing, and leadership.
For each principle, I'll provide specific tactics, techniques, and
practices we've developed to bind our company ever more tightly
to our reason for being. These include communications methods,
methods of handling on-the-job conflict, fiscal systems that support high performance, and leadership and training tools.

I hope you'll find these ground-level tools useful, either out
of the box or modified to fit your organization. I can't promise
you a dynamic culture and an ecstatic, engaged workforce overnight, but I do feel confident that a good deal of what worked for
us can work for you, too, helping you to transform your ordinary
organization into something truly extraordinary, inspiring, and
successful.

The tools I present are vitally important, but they aren't the essence of building a culture, any more than a particular move-ment or posture is the essence of tae kwon do. Rather, building a culture around a purpose is the task of becoming ever more cognizant of your organization, delving just a bit deeper into it, and becoming more and more self-aware of what you actually do.

Pursuing a purpose is like martial arts or yoga; it's some-thing done on a regular basis in an ongoing and never-ending attempt at mastery. There's nothing new in a conceptual sense about running a purpose-focused business; people talk about that all the time. What's new at Nick's is that the concepts aren't just talk around here. Thanks to our innovative tools, purpose is built into our business, woven into the fabric of the organization, day after day. And because we focus on grafting transformative practices into our operations, our culture has endured beyond the momentary intention and effort of individuals, even during those scary months in 2011.

LEARNING TO TRUST . . . AND TRACK

Aligning an organization and a culture around a purpose implies a wide-ranging shift in how we manage people. Despite all the talk about enlightened cultures, most workplaces still operate according to a command-and-control model. Bosses at your typical movie theater, hair salon, clothing boutique, or doctor's office stand over workers, telling them what to do and monitor-ing their activities. It's management by fear, and it winds up stifling the creativity of individual team members. Pursuing purpose frees an organization from command and control, grad-ually moving it toward a different system: what Bo Burlingham has called Trust and Track.

If managers implement the principles in this book, not only will their organizations shape their cultures by disciplining themselves around a purpose or reason for being; organizations will also teach individual team members, from management on down, a discipline they can then practice on the job and continue to practice in their personal lives. For instance, to help engender intensity around customer service, we train team members to do five things minute-to-minute in their work: greet guests every time they enter and exit the restaurant; subject anything they do or say to the Grandma Test (that is, would your grandmother approve of it?); answer the phone within three rings; help teammates at every opportunity ("it's not my job" is not in our vocabulary); and wave and smile at any guest who appears within five steps, no matter what the team member happens to be doing.

Think how difficult it would be to perform these five things consistently during your workday. These exhibitions of courtesy and respect are not something most of our team members do instinctively, but through continual practice, they come to internalize them as a discipline to the point where they become second nature.

If you commit yourself to pursuing purpose—and in a larger sense, culture—you'll discover, as we did, that your company is really a school disguised as a business, a school that enriches team members by teaching them discipline. When team members come to work, they focus every day on understanding the Nick's Experience just a little bit better and living it just a little bit more. Yet the test of this discipline is how well it endures *without* a manager standing over people telling them what to do. For a business to organize around purpose, the vast majority of its people must strive to live out that purpose with all their heart and soul. And people don't do that unless the reason for being comes from within, just as our organizational purpose comes from the inside out.

People will mess up—which is why companies must have mechanisms in place to track performance and take corrective action when team members stray off course (and why they must also take far more care to hire well than they otherwise would). But fundamentally, we trust people and give them sufficient space to live out the Nick's Experience in a unique way that meshes with their individuality. It's a manner of conducting a business that leads directly to higher performance. While results under command and control are usually limited by the manager's talent and preestablished norms, purpose-focused individuals who operate under the Trust and Track philosophy are free to tap the full breadth of their intrinsic motivations and abilities. People and teams can reach higher, previously undefined levels of performance—and so can the organization.

MOBILIZING OUR BETTER NATURES

This book has been born of lofty intentions. In detailing my company's own tried-and-true tools for building a high-performance culture, I hope to help a wide range of individual businesses and other organizations achieve higher performance. I also hope to change the way both employees and managers in our society think and feel about work. When organizations vigilantly pursue a higher purpose, work becomes an enjoyable part of life, a source of positive energy rather than a vortex that sucks energy out of you. We've got people who don't want to leave our restaurants when their shifts are over and who actually look forward to coming to work because they know they'll enjoy the experience. I've heard that, in a total reversal of the usual state of things, some moms who work for us come because it gives them strength to face some of the tough days they have with their kids. Imagine that!

I also want to provide an alternative to the lack of dignity and respect for fellow humans I encounter in many workplaces. Whatever else a high-performance culture does, it makes the workplace kinder. It fosters community spirit and empathy, because teammates at all levels feel connected around a common purpose. In a well-defined, vigorously maintained culture, we feel we're in it together, serving a cause that transcends any of us. We trust each other, because we understand each other and our commonalities, not merely our differences, and because the organization believes in our differences as sources of strength.

Culture and purpose are organic things and thus difficult to reduce to an analytic structure such as a book. When dealing with those two intangibles, everything relates to everything else; change one thing, and you change other things, too, sometimes without even knowing it. Many leaders reading a book like mine embrace one idea or tool that resonates, apply it at work, and leave the rest of the ideas and tools behind. Likewise, companies trying to build strong cultures often reform one part of the business, such as hiring or performance evaluation, and stop there. While I understand that some ideas and tools I offer will pique readers' interest more than others, this is not a choose-your-own-adventure type book. To get meaningful results, you really have to commit yourself to doing many things at once in the best way you can. Of course, mastering the art of doing this will take time, but you need to immerse yourself fully in the 360-degree discipline of building a culture from the get-go.

I hope you'll feel inspired enough to finish this book and

then go off to spread the word and make concrete changes. If I do my job right, this book will give entrepreneurs and corporate leaders the resources they need to generate a business plan for building purpose into their companies. Managers and CEOs will realize there are steps they can take to build more enriched and aligned workforces, no matter the size of their business or their industry. And students will understand how to build not merely a business but happier, more fulfilling careers aligned with their own purposes.

I end this introduction with a final thought. When I first started Nick's Pizza & Pub, people didn't only tell me I'd fail. They said I would need to work 24/7 to make sure the business was performing well because my employees wouldn't care so long as they got paid at the end of the week. These cynics told me I couldn't trust anybody, that people would steal from me, that I needed to stand over them and watch them like a hawk. I didn't believe these things. Instead, I believed that if people were trained right and you took care of them, they would do the right thing for both themselves *and* the business. People don't naturally wake up in the morning and say to themselves, "I'm going to sleepwalk through work and disappoint and betray my bosses today" (though they may do just that if they hate their jobs). If we can create positive cultures that promote their desires and personalities, they will wake up hoping to do something meaningful.

Today, after fifteen years in business, I stand by my original beliefs, because I've seen the dynamic of purpose play out before my eyes. As I detail for you the nuts and bolts of our high-performance culture, I hope I will also convey something of the joy, the love, and the fulfillment that surrounds the pursuit of purpose and the proliferation of trust in the workplace. With these elements in your possession, the only thing you'll still need to make an inspiring culture a reality is a fearless, thoughtful, and committed leader.

In other words, you!

CHAPTER ONE
Know What You're All About

If you want your company's culture to retain coherence over time, you must make sure it has a center, an organizing principle around which everything makes sense and everyone can rally. This center isn't an individual, or a product, or a physical location—in fact, it's not a physical thing at all. As I said in the Introduction, people do their best work when they have a higher purpose, and the same applies to organizations. Your purpose is the center of the culture that drives your business.

What do I mean by purpose? A purpose is a statement of what your company is all about. The purpose statement flows directly from the founder and others in the company, expressing their intense passion for the business as well as their unique perspective on the world.

Before I delve further into what a purpose is and how a company can define it, I want to discuss what a purpose *isn't*. A purpose is neither a mission nor a vision. Mission statements are typically goal-oriented. Citigroup's mission as of this writing is in part to "create the best outcomes for our clients and customers," while that of the CVS drugstore chain is to be "the easiest pharmacy retailer for customers to use." Vision statements are also goal-oriented, but they're typically a bit clearer about specific end states—fiscal, production, or competitive goals—that a company seeks to realize in a set period of time. Avon's vision is to be "the company that best understands and satisfies the product, service and self-fulfillment needs of women—globally," while the Alzheimer's Association's is "a world without Alzheimer's disease."

Purpose statements, by contrast, are sharp, present-centered statements of what the organization *already is right now* on days when everything works as it should. They embody a shared understanding of what a company is in business to do. Unlike vision or mission, which can reflect a strategic initiative, purpose flows directly out of emotional energy, the raw passion that team members apply as they run the business at its best. If we take time to know what we're about, distilling our purpose into a concise statement and creating a definitive list of supporting values, we can channel raw passion into a vibrant culture, unleashing the talents of our people and letting their best selves emerge.

When a company has a purpose, work becomes more meaningful. Innovation and creativity skyrocket, and people grow to trust their coworkers and managers more. The environment becomes more collaborative and communal and attrition plummets. This is especially valuable today when businesses around the world are under more pressure to attract and retain the best people, those who will actually help the organization perform better. Information technologies help us operate more efficiently, but a positive work environment born of higher meaning helps us attain whole new levels of off-the-charts performance.

How do we define off-the-charts performance? I like to think of that term as describing, beyond any objective measures, instances of peak experience, times when everything just seems to come together. During these moments, you reach heights as a team that nobody would have thought possible and that no individual team member—including the founder—could have realized alone. At these times, individual team members make a difference in the world and forge an emotional connection with other team members, the community, and guests.

Off-the-charts performance is ultimately quite mysterious; we don't understand its workings, and we can't just create it out of thin air. In most companies, it happens by accident, *despite* the company culture. But at Nick's, we open the door to it, foster the conditions that support it, and make it a focus of our day-to-day operations. By following a purpose, we create the potential for frequent peak experiences. If we don't follow a purpose, we pretty much guarantee we won't have too many peak experiences, or at least not as many as we might have had.

I know I've talked about how purpose comes from within, but it's important to understand that purpose is ineffective if it stays there. In some cases, a business might have a purpose, but it's hazy or vague or understood only by the founder or manager. That's not good enough. If your purpose isn't crystal clear in a language anybody can understand and if you don't articulate it to all of your people, it's useless. If you don't define what it means to act based on the company's purpose, teammates and management will have no way of knowing when they veer in the wrong direction. By failing to communicate, you might even inadvertently be signaling different purposes to different people, which can lead to tumult or, at the very least, stagnation. Taking time to craft a purpose is thus an essential first step to creating the culture we *want*, not merely contenting ourselves with the culture we already have.

DROWNING IN SUCCESS

Nick's didn't have a consciously articulated purpose and values when we first opened. Like many start-ups, we operated intuitively, and I was so grateful to be in business that I wanted to hug every guest who walked through the door. This passion impelled me to make sure that every guest was having a great time and feeling at home—that our small, close-knit team was delivering on my personal purpose of providing a fun, family-focused dining experience. I didn't realize it at the time, but I was naturally organizing my every move around fulfilling the purpose I had in opening the business. I was doing it in a fairly structured way, too, minute-to-minute, for I'd become accustomed to discipline based on the intense training I'd had playing football and wrestling in high school. Others working around me saw how I was behaving, and most of them in turn aligned themselves with our purpose.

Rather than articulating a clear set of values, I tried my best to apply some basic ideas I'd learned from my dad. He grew up poor in Chicago's Taylor Street neighborhood, one of five boys my grandma Theresa raised on her own. Lacking even a high school education, he started a series of businesses and always found a way to provide for his family—not just his wife and us three kids, but my grandma and from time to time one or more of my four uncles. While working for Village Pizza, Dad's pizza restaurant, and before that for his aluminum-siding business, I noticed how generous he was with his employees, how he was always straight with people, and how he treated customers like they were royalty. As a direct, gruff Italian guy, he could be swearing in a good-natured way at my cousin for a mistake he'd made, yet when customers came in, he'd bend over backward to treat them with the kindness, politeness, and good cheer they deserved. My dad adhered to other principles, too: Work hard; be dependable; trust nobody; minimize theft; be creative; and feel certain in your ability to solve any problem that might crop up. He was pretty successful, taking his last business, Village Pizza, from $10,000 in weekly sales to $25,000 over a five- to six-year period and enjoying the loyalty of a core of dedicated employees.

When I was twelve, my father took our family to Disney World. As we walked around, Dad commented on all the business details that made the place successful, especially the cleanliness and the precision with which it operated. Just how well the theme park was run came through one morning at breakfast when we witnessed an accident and its aftermath. Goofy was next to our table, and as he swung his head, his big floppy ear hit a light on the wall and broke it. Just a few minutes later, a maintenance man appeared from out of nowhere to replace the broken light with a new one. My dad was amazed, and so was I. At that breakfast, I resolved that someday I too would have a business that ran with this kind of attention to detail, efficiency, and cleanliness. Heck, maybe I'd even have my own version of Goofy.

During the first years of Nick's, my dad came by often to eat and hang out in the restaurant, and he never hesitated to offer me his version of "constructive" criticism about topics such as how we organized our menu, how we purchased food supplies, and how we managed and compensated team members. He was pretty good at identifying areas for improvement, and as I listened, I achieved amazing success. Sales doubled between 2000 and 2002, going from $1 million to $2 million, with margins staying roughly constant. By 2002 I had invested about $1 million to double the size of my restaurant and almost triple the seating capacity.

The reason: Customers were waiting two hours for a table, and we were turning away large groups of twenty, thirty, or more. I had tons of cash on hand, and at times I struggled to figure out what to do with the more than $100,000 in my bank account. Team spirit was high, with attrition below 100% annually, much less than the industry average of between 150% and 200%.*

I might have continued running my business indefinitely according to my father's principles were it not for a deep internal conflict I experienced. By 2001, almost seven years into my business, I still loved my restaurant, but something was missing, and I had a nagging sense we weren't reaching our full potential. What I couldn't quite bring myself to acknowledge was that I had been injecting too much of my father and not enough of *myself* into our operations. In particular, I didn't like how I was relating with our team members. Dad had long been cynical about people, taking their laziness and lack of dependability for granted. Like him, I took financial care of people who worked for me, yet I was a demanding, impatient boss who suffered no fools. Having cut my leadership teeth on construction sites, I read team members the riot act when things went wrong, a couple of times even bringing servers and bartenders to tears.

My dissatisfaction extended beyond Nick's. By the late 1990s, my wife and I weren't getting along. I was avoiding her, and the more she complained, the more I stayed away. I threw my energy into the restaurant, and I started hanging out with friends in my old Chicago neighborhood, playing poker, smoking cigars, and drinking beer until the early-morning hours. I

....

* That's right, most restaurants turn over their entire workforce as often as twice a year. These numbers do tend to get better during a recession, when people are grateful to have jobs, however unsatisfying those jobs may be.

still enjoyed coaching my kids in football and wrestling; sometimes I drove home at 5 A.M. on a Sunday for a 7 A.M. wrestling
meet after staying up all night. It got so bad that I would fall
asleep while I was driving. My kids would say, "Oh, yeah, this is
the stoplight where Daddy always takes a nap."

I had nowhere to turn. I couldn't talk to my father about
personal issues or lovey-dovey, self-reflective stuff. In Italian
American families like ours, fathers and sons aren't supposed to
share their feelings or spend a lot of time analyzing them. I knew
my dad loved me, but our way of bonding was to give each other
shit and talk about business problems or ideas. I had a couple of
buddies with whom I could vent, and I told them that something
was missing in my business and that I wasn't happy in my marriage, but none of them had any answers.

Things came to a head early one morning in June 2001. I
had stayed up late with my friends and was driving my new,
$100,000 Mercedes to a high school where they were holding a
wrestling tournament for my son's team. I fell asleep on the inter-
state doing ninety and woke up only when I bumped a minivan
in front of me. I swerved hard to the right, and the next thing I
knew, everything was dark and I smelled burning rubber. I tried
to open the driver's-side door, but as I cracked it open and
looked down, I could see the road was still moving.

Finally the car stopped, and I got out. I had driven under-
neath a moving gasoline tanker, and my car was lodged under-
neath the back wheels. The truck driver had pulled over onto the
shoulder and stopped, taking my car with him. Miraculously, I
wasn't hurt. I looked around the scene, concerned that I had
hurt someone else. When I went to check on the people in the
minivan, they gave me funny looks but said they were fine. Then
I went over to the trucker, asking, "Hey, are you okay?"

He too gave me a funny look. "Am *I* okay? The question is are *you* okay? Your car is totaled. I can't believe you walked away from that!"

For the next few days, what I had been through didn't register. Only about a week or two later did I wake up and say to myself: "What the hell am I doing here? Look at what my life has become." I began to think about what was wrong with a business and a marriage that on the outside seemed to embody the American dream but on the inside felt considerably less than satisfying.

It took me about a year to decide to get divorced. During that time, I kept working at my restaurant, and I made great strides figuring out how to make the business more fulfilling. I kept asking myself, "What is success? How can I make my work more successful—on *my* terms?" An epiphany came one busy Friday night while I was working a shift. I was standing by the fireplace in the middle of the dining room, surrounded by tons of happy people. Entire families were laughing and having fun. Tyler, a little boy with brown hair and a big grin on his face, ran up and said, "Hi, Nick!" I looked over at his family and waved, recognizing them as regulars who came in every Friday. "Wow," I thought, "look at what's going on here. These people aren't just feeling good; they're feeling good together. This is honest, healthy community. This is what America needs more of. How can I not bring this to other towns?"

What I'd realized, standing there in that dining room, was that my initial purpose—hazily articulated, to be sure—had been worth striving for, and that if I really wanted to push it ahead, there was more work to be done. I had opened Nick's without any idea of turning it into a chain—Dad had always sternly counseled against expansion. But now I realized that growth could be an exciting new mission for me, one that would allow me to rediscover my own company on a deeper level. Work could be meaningful again, and I could reconnect with my own passion and energies.

When I mentioned the possibility of expansion to my dad a week or two later, he was dead set against it. "I don't care for all those big companies. They don't do things right. They get bigger, and they don't care about what they do, and the customer experience goes down the tubes. I don't think you can have more than just one or two restaurants without changing your operations. And if you do have two, you'll just be killing yourself."

I thought about this for a moment. "You know, Dad, you're wrong. It *is* possible to expand and keep things right. It doesn't have to be one or the other. The key is to not try to control everything. I'm going to teach the *team* to run the company."

He laughed and shook his head. "Nicky, c'mon, gimme a friggin' break. You can't let the inmates steer the ship. They don't give a shit about shit." He smacked me on the shoulder. "You know what they give a shit about? Themselves. Making the dollars. What you need isn't teaching. It's security cameras and locks on the doors."

I didn't believe that for a second. Early in my career as a union carpenter, I'd had the bad luck of working under a foreman who yelled all the time and in general behaved like a total jerk. Nobody had anything nice to say about him, and when he wasn't around, the guys would sabotage his work. A few months later, the company assigned us a new foreman. Wayne, a former college fullback, was an inspirational leader. Sure, he was demanding, but where the old guy had led by instilling fear, Wayne did it by convincing us all that we, both individually and as a team, could conquer the world. And as a result, we upped our game, because deep down we really did care about doing a good job. The sabotage stopped, our better natures came out, and our performance improved.

In the past, I would have let my dad's comments go without taking issue, but not this time. "Dad," I said, "people *do* care— I've seen it. A lot of the people who work here really do want to do a good job. So I'm telling you, we can expand without compromising. We just need to learn how."

A LEAP OF FAITH

At the very least, I knew expansion would require creating scalable operational systems in our business. That was beyond my capability, so I searched for consultants who could help. The first three I interviewed didn't impress me; like my father, they were bottom-line thinkers who took a severe command-and-control approach and advised me to install security cameras to monitor employees. Then in the fall of 2001 I met the inspiring, inimitable Rudy Miick. During our initial conversations, he talked as though he'd been reading my mind and told me I needed to connect more with what was in my gut. Unlike everyone else I'd spoken to, Rudy described the *potential* of the team we had in place rather than its deficiencies. We all could be working better together, he insisted; the goal was to improve performance and prime us for growth by unleashing our talents and energies. Also, Rudy didn't try to fit me into some cookie-cutter model. Instead, he said that he wanted to serve as a partner with me and that together we'd figure out what worked. This was exactly what I needed.

I also chose Rudy because according to all my research, he knew how to build operational systems in restaurants better than anyone. Rudy came out and toured our site. We started by planning basic operational improvements, revamping our system of making our purchasing decisions, and beginning the task of mapping systematized processes for literally everything our people did on the job. These changes were far-reaching and quite foreign, and I did have doubts early on. But in the end, I decided to trust Rudy and implement all his suggestions to the letter.

During our conversations, Rudy emphasized the importance of bringing the entire business in line with the passion I held in my gut. He didn't use the word "purpose" at first; he simply said I needed to communicate my shared expectations for the business and for our team so everyone could understand them and work better to support an explicit, high-performance culture. When Rudy eventually did talk in earnest about purpose, he proposed that I organize our first-ever off-site corporate retreat. We'd gather together selected team members from across the organization and put the company's purpose in writing. The idea seemed strange, even a little frightening: two long days of sitting in a circle and talking honestly about our business, even the bad stuff. There would be flip charts, creative projects with Play-Doh and markers, meditations, and, of course, that all-too-scary thing: emotions.

I was a pretty private person and not the slightest bit New Agey. Where I come from, people in a small business don't go off in the woods to talk—not while there are paying customers back in the store waiting to be served. When my dad heard about the idea, he almost choked on his Italian beef sandwich. "You're going to do *what*? Pay people to talk? What for? What do you gain by having everyone sit around and talk about the jobs they do? They just need to get their asses to work."

My dad is hardly alone in this perspective. Many of today's leaders believe you shouldn't solicit the opinions of the people who work for you, because what they think doesn't matter. In the minds of such leaders, companies should be run by benevolent dictators. Good old-fashioned command and control. Well, for us at least, that was about to change. Whether Dad liked it or not.

"Let's do it," I told Rudy. I was nervous, but I trusted him. There was something about Rudy—not just what he said, but his whole manner, his way of being—that made me want to keep going down this path and find out what this purpose-related stuff was all about. To prepare for the retreat, I carefully selected a "slice team" of servers, bartenders, cooks, busboys—two people from every work group, a newbie and a veteran—as well as our entire management team. Taking off our aprons, putting down our knives and our dish towels, we joined Rudy and an associate for what would become a life- and business-altering experience.

GETTING IN TOUCH WITH OUR PURPOSE—AND OURSELVES

Once we got settled at the retreat, we examined our purpose by analyzing as closely as possible what our company was doing *right*—the essence of the value we were adding, the contribution we were making to our customers, the need we were filling in the community. We told stories about what our guests were saying, and we spent even more time probing our own feelings. What made us feel good about the restaurant? What were we as individuals most passionate about? How did we define ourselves?

We discovered that we felt less like a group of colleagues and more like a family that worked together. We also discussed the impact we were having in the community by donating money and supporting kids' sports teams. And we talked about how casual and fun the restaurant was, with peanut shells on the floor and the sound of everyone socializing. This discussion was an emotional exercise, not merely or primarily a rational one. We were working hard to get in touch with our souls—and the soul of our company—and to put that into words. I hadn't realized it before, but on the deepest level purpose is a spiritual thing. And the experience of putting purpose together was spiritual too, not just a typical day at the office when we're talking about numbers.

Most organizations shy away from emotions. We feel uncomfortable exposing ourselves to our colleagues, and it's probably fair to say that most people on the job don't even know how to do it. Yet a company's purpose can't just be about the bottom line or financial incentives. To inspire outstanding performance, an organization's purpose has to touch something deep inside us. As Rudy realized so well, bringing out the best in people means laughing, crying, sweating, feeling uncomfortable, and allowing the words capturing our purpose to flow from there.

Emotions ratcheted up as the hours ticked by. We made utter fools of ourselves with Play-Doh and art exercises. We also made ourselves vulnerable by talking frankly about our deficiencies. I took the lead by owning up to my tendency to reprimand teammates in front of others or show favoritism to my sister or a cute server. I was also sad and embarrassed to hear about the negative impact I'd had on my colleagues. As one of the participants told me, "You used to be nice to me, but now it seems I can never please you." Another said, "I never hear what I'm doing well, just what I'm doing wrong. You never seem to have anything nice to say to me." In the face of such withering criticism, I was tempted to shut the conversation down, to throw around my authority as the boss. But I didn't. I had committed myself to

Rudy's process, and I was determined to see it through. At the end of the first day, I was wiped out, even though I hadn't done anything physical.

During this first day, we wrote down ideas we'd brainstormed on flip boards—lists of words that described what the restaurant meant to us, phrases describing positive elements of Nick's, and, on one board, a formula: "Family + Fun + People + Giving + Good Food." On the second day, we honed all this down into one statement, our purpose statement. From a long series of paragraphs, we arrived at a one-page document. And then, over many hours, we reduced that to a single sentence written in the present tense, choosing each word with care. We worked until we felt we could all agree on how each word made us feel. Even the semicolon and exclamation point in our statement mattered and required consensus.

OUR PURPOSE

THE NICK'S EXPERIENCE

Our dedicated family provides *this* community an unforgettable place; to connect with your family and friends, to have fun, and to feel at home!

Our final purpose statement begins with "our family" because, first and foremost, we felt like a family. That was easy. We *as a family* were providing a place for other families. Then we added "dedicated" because we agreed that when we each came to work, we wanted to do our best. We could also agree that Nick's was an extraordinary, unique, unforgettable place. Our building was an old barn, hand-built and designed by me and furnished with antiques—it really was "unforgettable." We chose "connect" because we all genuinely cared about guests who came in the door; we didn't talk to them just because we needed their dollars. Also, we wanted our restaurant to serve as a place where families could "connect" with one another, without distraction. We weren't doing Chuck E. Cheese, with mascots running around, and we weren't handing out crayons to distract the little kids, either. Our place was about people spending quality time interacting with other people in their lives.

More specifically, the Nick's Experience was about *enjoying* the time one spent in our restaurant—hence the words "have fun" and "feel at home." I had opened Nick's because I wanted kids to be kids, to relax and have fun without parents having to worry that they were causing a scene or bothering other customers. By design, our place felt like home—soft lighting, warm fireplace, open floor plan, even a game room. We had an antique phone booth that kids could go into and old cigarette machines on which they could tug. Moreover, we ourselves were having fun. As a team, we were relaxed, not full of ourselves, not yelling and screaming at one another (except for me, on occasion). Finally, and paradoxically, we were serious about having fun and feeling at home, which is why we capped off the statement with an exclamation point.

FROM PURPOSE TO VALUES

After the session, we took our newly defined purpose statement back to the restaurant. I printed it out, put it on plaques, and told the team members who didn't attend the retreat how excited each of us was about it. About six weeks later, we held a second retreat to define more detailed company values that related to the purpose. Just as Congress writes laws that help translate the more abstract Constitution into practical terms, so too our stated values would help make the purpose real (giving rise in turn to specific principles and operational processes). I like to say that the purpose is the "why" and the values are the "how" of our operations. The values serve as guidelines for making practical decisions every day.

The process of generating values was similar to that used in our first retreat. We involved most of the same people, and once again we dug deep into our emotions, this time looking more intensely at the specifics of performance. Our task was to figure out how we delivered our purpose every day and what set us apart as a company. We began by working with a list we'd generated of key elements of our operations that are important to us, with Rudy helping us to check these for their broader impact on the company and its purpose.

One of the first potential pairs of values we came up with was "dignity and respect." We all agreed that everyone in the company—from the dishwasher to the head bartender—should be treated as equals. Our team said they found it amazing that I brought out a sandwich for the truck drivers who delivered our food. "Of course," I said, "we have to treat them well, too!"

Next on our list was "ongoing learning and teaching." Already, our teammates benefited from an extraordinary amount of teaching and learning—more than at most restaurants, and indeed most companies. A general atmosphere of learning and growth pervaded our work; I've always expected everyone to help one another (including myself) develop on the job, helping their teammates cut pizzas or serve guests better.

Nick's Values

- We treat everyone with dignity and respect.

- We are dedicated to the learning, teaching, and ongoing development of each other.

- We have fun while we work!

- We provide a clean and safe environment for our guests and team members.

- We honor individual passions, and creativity at work and at home.

- We communicate openly, clearly, and honestly.

- We honor the relationships that connect our team, our guests and community.

- We take pride in our commitment to provide quality service and a quality product.

- We celebrate and reward accomplishments and "A+" players.

- We support balance between home and work.

- Health: We are a profitable and fiscally responsible company. We support the physical and emotional well-being of our guests and team members.

- Our team works through support and cooperation.

I won't comment at length on each of our values. Some, such as having fun or pursuing individual passions, appeared obvious to everyone at the retreat; you can't have a fun family environment if the team members in charge of supporting it aren't having fun and acting naturally themselves. Since we are a family restaurant, clearly we should "provide a clean and safe environment." "Communicate openly, clearly, and honestly" made sense because we had always felt it was important not to keep secrets around the company's performance and because the drama and gossip that follows from keeping secrets would likewise inhibit the atmosphere of family comfort we were trying to achieve. We'd always been known for offering the highest-quality food products available, so "quality service" and "a quality product" were a no-brainer.

By contrast, "A+ players" was not obvious. I knew that sometimes I followed in my dad's footsteps and didn't always celebrate other peoples' superior performance as well as I could. This was something I wanted to get better at, something I aspired to make a part of our company's culture as a whole. On the other hand, we didn't want to specify too closely what "high performance" was, because in a learning organization, the performance bar is constantly inching upward. If we defined performance now, we would foreclose on performance that in the future was even better. Thus we left it purposely vague: "A+" performance.

In addition to helping our company identify the better parts of our nature that we wanted to develop further, Rudy also helped us sharpen our thinking about values we did already understand and accept. The second-to-last value, "health," is a good example. We talked about physical health

a bit, how I encouraged people to go to health clubs, play softball with one another, go to yoga, or train in the martial arts. Sep-
arately, we talked about profitability and fiscal responsibility.
But we'd never thought to bring the two together. Rudy helped
us see that physical health and financial health were both part of
being responsible to ourselves for our own well-being.

You'll notice on our list that we didn't number our values.
That's because we didn't want to suggest that one particular
value outweighed any other. All were important and of equally
high priority. We used the present tense because we wished to
convey that each value exists in the here and now, and that
employees should be keeping all of them in mind at all times. As
we'll see later in the book, we track and celebrate behavior that
aligns with our values in the moment, and we correct actions
inconsistent with our values in the moment as well. If I see something as simple as a team member saying "Thank you" or "I'm
coming up behind you" as he or she passes, I'll recognize that
behavior by saying, "That's the way to support our value of dignity and respect!" (usually with a big smile and thumbs-up).
Our values are descriptions of our intended behavior right now,
not goals we'll achieve someday.

TOWARD YOUR OWN PURPOSE AND VALUES

Defining purpose and values is a major task, so it's important to
take the time to do it right. If you are as much in the dark about
your purpose as we were, I strongly advise you to work with an
experienced consultant like Rudy who can take you through the
process. I can't tell you how valuable it was to have an outside
person in the room to listen and help parse what we were saying.

Now, I recognize that this is an investment. If you don't have the capital right now, or if you'd like to at least get started on your own, there are easy exercises you can do to jump-start your thinking. Here's where we take out a piece of paper and pencil and get cracking.

The first step: Understand the need to craft a purpose for yourself. Perhaps you're not convinced your organization has an issue with purpose. You have a mission statement, right? It's posted right up there on the wall. In fact, your organization might well be aligned right now around a purpose. But let's make sure. To understand how well your firm expresses your own sense of personal purpose, perform the following brief assessment:

1. How would I rate the company's financial success against my expectations?
2. On a scale of 1 to 10, how happy am I to come into work each day?
3. On a scale of 1 to 10, how happy are my employees to come to work each day?
4. On a scale of 1 to 10, how much value does my firm contribute to the larger community?
5. On a scale of 1 to 10, to what extent does my workforce push toward a single, unified goal?
6. Overall, how would I rate the performance of individuals and teams within my company?
7. How would I rate the performance of the worst team within my organization?
8. How would I rate the performance of our worst individuals relative to the competition?

How did you score? Is there work to be done? If the answer
is yes, continue on with me as we begin to conceptualize a
purpose for your company. As I've said, a purpose is essentially
a statement that describes an organization's reason for being. On
a sheet of paper, answer the question "Why does this company
exist?" If you're the company's founder, you might wish to think
about the original motives and passions you had when starting
the company. What was it that got you out of bed in the morning
during those early days (besides terror at the possibility of
failing)? If you're not the founder, you might conduct this exercise with the founder. If you're the head of a division in a larger
company, understanding the company's purpose can help
you understand the division's purpose.

Passion is the place to start, but a company's unstated purpose is meaningful only to the extent that it's expressed in
tangible form. To further understand and refine what your purpose might be—in particular, to determine the strengths that are
firmly in place—take some time to observe and analyze your
company's presence in the community. What are your buildings
like inside and out? What kinds of marketing do you do? What
kind of figure do you cut in the community? We'll talk in later
chapters about how to bring the entirety of your business in line
with purpose, but for now, pay close attention to the outward-
facing parts that just "feel right." Consider too your company's
internal landscape. What do your teams look like? How are your
work groups organized? What key business practices do you follow? How do you finance operations? When assessing these
various internal elements, you'll naturally find parts you like and
parts you don't like. What sort of purpose statement do the positive or desirable ones lend themselves to?

Another thing you can do right now to better grasp your purpose is to consider how you serve the wider world. In my mind, purpose connects intimately with sustainability. Think about how your operations contribute to sustainability in the following areas: (1) environment, (2) society, (3) your local community, (4) the company, and (5) individual team members. What impact are you having? What are you especially proud of? What efforts would you like to emphasize more in the future?

As you run through these exercises, you're simply trying to begin to generate language and concepts around your purpose. Take your time here. Come back to these questions on several occasions over different days. Do your responses differ from session to session? Do they evolve? Are there recurring themes? Don't just write down your responses; spend time evaluating them, interpreting them, wondering about them, discussing them with others. Mark up your notes, circling key concepts and phrases. Then brainstorm anything you can think of that has to do with these key concepts. You're trying to access your passions here, but you're also simultaneously trying to understand and communicate them to the outside world, and that requires a great deal of honest reflection.

Let's say you've spent time hashing around ideas. How do you finalize the statement itself? Here's the really hard part. You've got to study each word, just as the team at Nick's did. Be precise. Go for words that capture the exact idea you're trying to convey. Borrowing from Rudy,* I'd recommend the following:

....

* For where the core of our hiring system started, go to http://www.miick.com/index .html.

- Use the first person in your statement (for example, "*Our* dedicated family").
- Use the present tense ("We change lives, create traditions, build community. . . .").
- Lose every unneeded word, and be sure to include the specific words you need to be absolutely clear.
- Beware using single words (for example, "honesty") as a purpose statement or as a value. Doing so generally betrays a lack of thought.
- Do away with any added syllable (choose "be reliable" instead of "depend on reliability"). You want your purpose statement to be as concise, clear, and simple as possible. Make every syllable count.
- Lose the negative and instead use positive language ("We create a sustainable, waste-free environment" as opposed to "We don't create waste or harm the environment").
- Be active and definitive. Don't use words like "commit," "commitment," "believe," "will," "intend," "endeavor," and "strive." Don't allow for any kind of wiggle room. Instead of "We strive to change lives, create traditions, build community . . ." say "We change lives, etc. . . ."
- Finally, employ aspirational language—words that lead you to change lives, build community, create new traditions, engage, inspire . . . *be!*

As you work on applying these suggestions, remember: Your goal in crafting a purpose statement isn't absolute grammatical perfection. Rather, it's to produce something that aligns as closely as possible with what you and your team feel in your hearts, as well as with who and what you are as people and personalities. You might arrive at words and grammar that aren't, strictly speaking, "correct," and that's okay. In fact, quirky, unorthodox language might be the best possible solution, the most authentic one.

If your words come from the gut rather than the head, as I'm suggesting, the final product—your purpose statement—will endure over time and withstand any impulse toward second-guessing. At one point a few years ago, we thought we had made a mistake by failing to include language about accountability in our purpose statement. As we thought about whether we wanted to insert something, we analyzed the purpose statement and decided "accountability" would be better communicated in our list of values, since these focus more on the "how." Then we realized our values already communicated accountability in the directness and clarity of their phrasing and in the inclusion of words like "commitment" and "dedicated." Time and again, I've found that when we revisit our purpose statement, it's only to go deeper, never to change anything. Mission (an aspiration you have for your company) might change, and vision (a specific goal your organization wishes to achieve) might change, but never purpose.

It continually amazes me how many different layers of meaning you can find in a well-done, rich purpose statement. Of course, having a good purpose statement doesn't mean you'll be a good company, and there are still plenty of companies out there that have missed the point about purpose—if they've bothered to look for it at all. Consider the following examples, big and small, across an array of industries.

COMPANY	PURPOSE STATEMENT?	COMMENT
BRITISH PETROLEUM	**Yes, but ...** "We help the world meet its growing need for heat, light and mobility. And we strive to do that by producing energy that is affordable, secure and doesn't damage the environment."	Good statement. Clear. Present-centered. But does it translate into action? Just because a company has a great purpose statement doesn't mean it will stick to it. Their use of the word "strive" already gives them a way out.
DOMINO'S PIZZA	**Unclear.** The company's Web site identifies Domino's as "one brand" that focuses on "putting people first," "demanding integrity," "striving for customer loyalty," etc.	Some room for improvement here. Domino's needs to search deeper to locate the one thing that defines what they do at their best. Domino's current language feels more like values than a unitary statement of purpose.
KIND HEALTHY SNACKS	**Yes.** "From crafting healthy & delicious award-winning products with all-natural ingredients you can see and pronounce to inspiring '*not* so random' acts of kindness, we strive to make this world a little kinder. We call this the **KIND** movement."	Love it. Talk about inspirational. How can you not feel passionate and engaged as you bite into their all-natural snack bars? Kind is a purpose-driven company—and they make sure you know it.
SOUTHWEST AIRLINES	**Yes and no.** To the best of my knowledge, Southwest doesn't have a purpose statement. They do have a "mission" statement that feels very much like a purpose statement: "The mission of Southwest Airlines is dedication to the highest quality of Customer Service delivered with a sense of warmth, friendliness, individual pride, and Company Spirit."	Pretty nice job articulating a purpose for a great company. What's missing is an active verb in the present tense, as well as some attempt to make it personal for people and a word like "we" that would evoke community. Other than that, I wouldn't change too much here.

Sources: www.bp.com; www.dominosbiz.com; http://kindsnacks.com; kind snacks product packaging; www.southwest.com.

BRINGING THE PURPOSE TO LIFE

A couple of weeks after finishing our values statement, we rolled out the purpose and values during an all-company meeting. Rudy had predicted that a contingent within the company would resist change, and he was right. One of our more vocal bartenders asked point-blank: "What is this shit?" Likewise, my dad wasn't too hot on the idea, and even years later he still isn't. While I was researching this chapter, he told me, "Look, you're in business to make money. Do you really think you're going to make more money because people like working here? If anything, purpose and values only apply to someone who is a little more intelligent. I guarantee you, if you cut back pay and benefits, you would have the same problems as anyone else. It's all about money."

It was hard for most of our team members to grasp the touchy-feely concepts of purpose and values, but within a few weeks, the resistance had died down. As Matt, one of our managers, remembers: "I realized that the culture had not really changed. Nick was always the culture, and what he did was make the culture he lived explicit."

Over the better part of a decade, we've settled in and worked hard to bring the purpose to life. We've revamped our marketing, recruiting, hiring, orientation, training, performance evaluation, and financial management, not to mention the way we organize and hold our meetings. It's no exaggeration to say that literally *everything* that goes on today at Nick's is designed to somehow push forward our stated reason for being. And the minute we discover that something or someone doesn't further that purpose, it's out the door.

Our transformation has been so thorough, and the passion

and performance of our workforce so high, that our values are now inscribed on our physical plant itself. At our original restaurant in Crystal Lake, an underground tunnel connects two basement areas to one another. A few years ago, Ali, a skinny, soft-spoken seventeen-year-old team member, suggested we paint our values on the tunnel wall. "Since the values guide us in how we make decisions," she reasoned, "why don't we let each new team member come down here and sign the wall under the value they connect with most? It could be part of the celebration of them being a team member at Nick's and becoming part of our family." That was one of the greatest ideas I'd ever heard of in support of the purpose—and one of many I didn't come up with myself.

An especially popular section of our basement tunnel.

We've seen in this chapter that defining purpose is an important step in transitioning your firm toward a high-performance, meaning-laden culture. Yet it's only the beginning. Purpose, you see, isn't ever finished; it's a business discipline rooted in passion that's practiced in an open-ended way by everyone in the company, including and especially the

CEO. By moving deliberately and uncompromisingly toward purpose, by subjecting everything in the firm to the test of whether it aligns with the company's purpose, you're assuring the company's success by steering the organization closer and closer to what it already is.

CHAPTER TWO
Get the Word Out

Building a high-performance culture—on both the individual and organizational levels—requires single-mindedness, intensity, and dedication on everyone's part. Only when your teammates adopt your purpose as their own will you be able to make a difference in your culture and your company. Therefore, it's not enough to just establish a purpose; you need to talk about it to your fellow team members—those responsible for representing you to your customers and employees. No, they don't have to be able to recite the purpose verbatim, but they should understand it, get behind it, even internalize it to the extent that it becomes second nature. In addition, you need to make sure they are *acting* on your reason for being each and every day.

Communicating the purpose often helps create a high-performance culture by making expectations clear. Experienced teammates come in with baggage from other jobs and careers—work habits, big and small, that prove inconsistent with your purpose. Even if these teammates want to change, they'll revert back to their habits if the company's reason for being is not defined for them at every turn. People new to the workforce, like the teenagers we hire as servers, hosts, and pizza makers, also will need minute-to-minute support as they train themselves to adopt your purpose as their own. Talking about your reason for being galvanizes excitement by conveying how important the purpose is to the organization. Communication builds cohesion, momentum, and a sense of identity by reaffirming the purpose as the sole collective benchmark around which team members will orient their behavior and attitudes.

The best kind of communication comes not through words but through action. Companies and individuals speak loudest through their examples—the actual operational systems, practices, and processes that shape the on-the-job experience. Since defining and rolling out our purpose, we've revamped how we operate to reflect, communicate, and support our reason for being. Some operational components—the two we'll talk about in this chapter, design of our physical space and our marketing—comprise the outward face we show the world. Yet the most important components are and always will be inward-facing, the stuff customers don't see but that make their time with us special and our company one worth working for. I'll detail those operational elements later in the book as I illustrate other governing principles for creating an inspirational, high-performance culture.

NEVER-ENDING CAMPAIGN

When we rolled out our purpose statement in June 2002, we unleashed an internal and external marketing campaign that continues today. We made big foam boards with the Nick's Experience purpose statement (and our values) printed on them and posted them every time we had a meeting and in our break area, where team members congregated throughout the day. We put plaques up where customers could see them. Then we started thinking of other places we could display the Nick's Experience, such as on our Web site and training materials. Today, you'll find our purpose statement in investor packets, press releases, business cards, e-mail signatures for our managers, promotional announcements, training materials, and teammate evaluations. It's also posted in high-traffic back-office areas like our break area and the entrance to our restaurants, on the cover sheet of our job applications, and on whiteboards at every meeting we hold, even off-site. You really can't have any kind of contact with our company without learning about the Nick's Experience, or at least that we have a purpose.

We have to saturate all stakeholders—from customers to employees to investors—because we can't take for granted that people will immediately "get" the Nick's Experience, or that they'll remember it from yesterday to today, from this morning to tonight. Remember, our goal is to engineer and build a culture, one that will inspire people to do their best for themselves and the company. We can't just let culture "happen." We have to mold it, shape it—take control of it—and that means repeating our mantra at every turn. We're always trying to think of new ways to communicate the purpose as our company changes and grows. T-shirts? Pens? Goodyear Blimps? The sky's the limit!

From the moment prospective Nick's team members walk in the door, they come face-to-face with the Nick's Experience— both in our job application form and in our orientation classes. If these applicants end up coming to work for us, they encounter the Nick's Experience in their day-to-day interactions with fellow employees and guests and through all of the training and advancement programs we have at Nick's. They probably also encounter the Nick's Experience during off-hours when they overhear guests in the community discussing our great service and friendly atmosphere—two key aspects of our overall purpose. As we've discovered, there is no clear "inside" and "outside" to the company when communicating purpose, no clear distinction between communications addressed to different stakeholders.

I'm emphasizing team members, but going hog wild in communicating our purpose helps underline to all stakeholders just how seriously we take it, and how unique we are as a business because of that. By posting the Nick's Experience purpose statement as well as a statement of our values at every entryway, not just a few of them, we're making it clear that our purpose is absolutely fundamental to us and our self-definition, and that you can expect to encounter the effects of it as you range more widely in our restaurants and our company and experience them more deeply. In some places, such as our Web site, we're quite explicit about the importance of purpose, using language like "Our company exists for one reason . . . " to introduce the purpose statement. We find it helpful to offer just a little bit of education about what a purpose is, and about our intention to be a purpose-driven company, so that people see that as our organization's defining quality.

When I walked through the door while touring one well-regarded company in my industry, I saw awards on the wall, but I saw their mission statement (forget about their purpose statement) posted only in a few cubicles, and not at all in the warehouse or the industrial kitchens. In the shipping and receiving area, I spotted a sign that stated the purpose, but it was hung way up high on the wall, where nobody could see it. You have to wonder: Is the purpose just window dressing? Does the company actually care about it? Are they really creating meaningful work? To me, a company like this is a "neck-up" organization that appeals to people intellectually but doesn't forge a deeper, sustainable, heartfelt bond that extends from employees to the larger community. Our goal in obsessively talking about our purpose and values is to make everybody understand that they aren't simply convenient slogans.

Talking endlessly about purpose is also vital in setting performance expectations. Because we print the Nick's Experience purpose statement on our menus, guests literally take it with them to their individual tables and so can keep it fresh in their minds during individual interactions with staff and our products. The team sees that we communicate our purpose to guests, and they realize how important it is that they perform within its context. When handing out job applications, our people make absolutely clear to prospective team members that our purpose is central to everything we do, telling them explicitly, "Read very carefully through our purpose statement and our values on the cover sheet. If you feel like this is something you want to be a part of, then continue on and fill out the application. If you don't feel right about it or if it doesn't make sense, that's okay too, but please just hand the application back." About 10% of applicants do hand it back, and that's fine. In the end, we don't care if someone is the greatest server, bartender, or pizza maker in Chicago. If they can't get behind the Nick's Experience, they won't be a positive addition to our team or culture.

By also defining the Nick's Experience on the cover of our training packet, we send the message that the purpose is even

---

Thank you for applying for a position on our team at Nick's Pizza & Pub!

We are ALWAYS looking for passionate, committed people who can deliver exceptional guest service. If you are "just looking for a job" Nick's is <u>NOT</u> the place for you! Please take a minute and read through this cover sheet prior to filling out your application. We take what is written here very seriously!!

OUR PURPOSE

"THE NICK'S EXPERIENCE"

OUR DEDICATED FAMILY PROVIDES THIS COMMUNITY AN UNFORGETTABLE PLACE; TO CONNECT WITH YOUR FAMILY AND FRIENDS, TO HAVE FUN AND TO FEEL AT HOME.

Our Values

- *We treat everyone with dignity and respect.*
- *We are dedicated to the learning, teaching, and ongoing development of each other.*
- *We have fun while we work!*
- *We provide a clean and safe environment for our guests and team members.*
- *We honor individual passions, and creativity at work and at home.*
- *We communicate openly, clearly and honestly.*
- *We honor the relationships that connect our team, our guests and community.*
- *We take pride in our commitment to provide quality service and a quality product.*
- *We celebrate and reward accomplishments and "A+" players.*
- *We support balance between home and work.*
- *Health: We are a profitable and fiscally responsible company. We support the physical and emotional well-being of our guests and team members.*
- *Our team works through support and cooperation.*

If this sounds like the kind of place you would like to work, then promptly fill out the attached application. If this sounds like a place that you may not be interested in, then kindly save yourself the time, and do not complete the application.

Thank you for your time!

By presenting our purpose and values front and center, we are also sending a strong message about what is important in our company.

more important than any of the specific tasks you might learn from what's printed inside the packet, such as how to flatten dough or answer the phone. And our purpose statement emerges once again in our performance evaluations, when we state explicitly that team members are held responsible for how well they've worked to help realize the Nick's Experience. (By the way, the higher up you get in our company, the deeper you're assessed based on the company's purpose statement. Our

360-degree evaluations assess executives, including myself, on their "pride in purpose and values," and how well that pride has become evident in specific actions and behaviors.)

I don't want you to get the idea that we're perfect at communicating the Nick's Experience. When I sat down to think about this chapter, I realized that our accounting department doesn't have purpose statements in their documents and workspaces; this is an area we'll need to address as we grow. (Our accounting department used to be one person, and now we're bringing in outside people trained as accountants, so we'll need to be more explicit about purpose in the future.) Also, our T-shirts don't have the Nick's Experience on it. How in the heck did I miss something so obvious? You can be sure I'll rectify that when we order the next batch.

Purpose isn't just another business initiative; it's something sacred you pursue with all your heart and soul. And indeed, when communicating the purpose statement we treat it as if it's a sacred text, not to be altered in any way. Recently, a blogger in the restaurant industry upset me by changing the purpose statement in an attempt to summarize it. Dude, are you crazy!? The Nick's Experience is the one thing that *can't* be changed, precisely because it was the product of a very intense and deliberate process. Think of it this way: You can change many kinds of recipes, but a cake recipe can't be altered without the cake suffering. I'm so vigilant on this point that when I recently discovered that an exclamation point was missing in our purpose statement as it appeared on our Web site, I immediately had that fixed.

KNOWING WHEN THEY "GET" IT

As I've mentioned, the main goal is to get team members to not just memorize the purpose statement but to internalize it, so that they can live it minute-to-minute.* But how do you know when that's happened? At Nick's, we embrace a common pedagogic model, conceiving a team member's alignment with our purpose and values in terms of four stages of competence:

- **Unconscious incompetence**, when team members don't know what to do to bring the purpose alive in a specific task, and they don't even know that they don't know.
- **Conscious incompetence**, when team members understand they're failing to execute a task based on purpose but haven't been able to fix the behavior yet.
- **Conscious competence**, when team members are capable of behaving based on the purpose statement but have to apply themselves consciously to do it.
- **Unconscious competence**, the highest stage, when, after much practice, team members execute tasks based on the purpose statement naturally and intuitively, as a reflex, often without even needing to think about it.

We conduct formal performance checks and evaluations to see if people are internalizing the Nick's Experience, yet such methods might not be the most effective way to know what's happening. In keeping with our aversion to a command-and-control philosophy, we feel it's best not to spend too much time telling people what to do or what words to say. We also know

....

* We don't expect our junior employees to repeat the purpose statement word for word and, as I'll explain, that's not necessary in order for them to be able to deliver on it. We do expect that trainers and salaried managers are able to recite the Nick's Experience purpose statement word for word.

that when team members know they are being evaluated, they will try to create an image of what they *think* you want to see, even if it doesn't reflect their normal behavior. We're aiming for something deeper: purpose coming from within, merged with the team member's unique individuality. For that you have to let go a little bit but simultaneously pay attention in a different way.

To test for unconscious competence, our managers and I look for clues in casual conversation—an individual's body movements, tone of voice, language, etc. With our executives, for instance, I'll track whether they use "I" or "we" in talking about our company as opposed to "they" or "you." A new executive might say at first, "This is how you do it here," but after weeks of immersion in our culture and effort on their part, they'll say, "This is how *we* do it," and apart from their actual on-the-job behaviors, that's one clue that they've unconsciously absorbed the Nick's Experience. Nonexecutive team members, in telling me about their day on the job, might say, "I had this customer" in casual conversation. I'll say, "A customer? Is that what you have at your own home—a customer?" "Guest," they'll say—a term much better aligned with our purpose. When they start saying "guest" on their own, automatically, I'll know that the Nick's Experience has become thoroughly embedded in their unconscious minds.

Another great way to detect whether the purpose is really sticking is to observe how people behave under stress. Our restaurants are packed on Friday and Saturday nights. If on those very busy and sometimes stressful nights I see individuals revert to behavior or speech that's inconsistent with the Nick's Experience (getting caught up in an argument or conflict with a guest, for instance), then I know they haven't internalized our reason for being as fully as they might. When team members can remember to greet everyone they see within five steps of them (one of the behaviors we train for) even when two new tables have just sat down and orders for two existing tables have come up at the same time, then I feel pretty sure that assimilation of the Nick's Experience is reaching the level of internalized competence.

To visualize the progress people are making in internalizing purpose, you might try placing it on a rough continuum. Visualize on the far left-hand side the novice team member whose language in both on-the-job and informal circumstances is totally unaligned with our purpose even in nonstressful situations. One notch to the right, we find team members whose language on the job is aligned under nonstressful circumstances, but whose conversation in informal situations reveals detachment from the purpose. Then, farther to the right, are team members whose work behavior and informal conversations are *partially* aligned under nonstressful circumstances. Even farther to the right are team members who have become fully aligned under nonstressful situations; then partially aligned under partially stressful conditions; then fully aligned under partially stressful; etc. Close to the far right-hand side, we find individuals who are fully aligned at all times and under all situations, inside and outside at work. Finally, we find people who are so aligned that they can track whether others around them are aligned as well.*

In Chapter Six, I'll describe how we use intensive monitoring and coaching of team member activity to align behavior ever more closely with the Nick's Experience. Mostly we try to intervene in a positive way, applauding team members on those occasions when

....

* This continuum model was inspired by a "synergy" model created for me by another consultant we've worked with, Christina Barr from Square One Solutions.

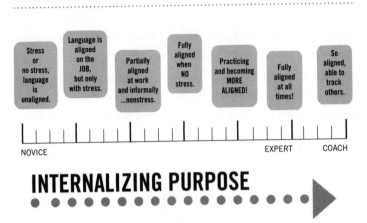

INTERNALIZING PURPOSE

they perform based on our purpose, so they'll feel motivated and inspired to get it right more often, even when nobody's looking. On occasions when team members fall short, we avoid dwelling on negativity or "criticism" of any kind. Instead, our managers and trainers build excitement around learning and growth, gently pointing team members to the opportunities at hand for getting their performance to an even higher level.

If you take care to surround team members with the purpose, getting most new hires to the "unconscious competence" level can happen relatively quickly—in my experience, within sixty to ninety days. The continuum helps along the way because it allows us to demarcate relative expectations for people at different levels. For instance, the sixteen-year-old who has never worked before will probably start much farther to the left than a fifty-year-old seasoned employee but will move to the right at a faster clip. Why? Because the fifty-year-old already has a well-developed sense of self and perhaps an ingrained cynicism about the workplace, and therefore may have difficulty truly integrating the purpose. Likewise, we can chart the relative progress of members of the same cohort. Not all sixteen-year-old team members are the same, nor are all twenty-two-year-olds; we've seen some young workers incorporate our purpose with blazing speed, and it's fun to see how differently they pick up new things.

Unconscious competence in a skill is a pretty big deal, and it's fulfilling for everyone when an individual attains it. Ben, one of our carry-out hosts and managers, puts it well: "For me, the best part about Nick's is the daily experience of learning and growing and building on what I already know. I feel most proud when I see another team member doing something unconsciously competent after they have been striving to do it for either months or years. Witnessing that moment when they do it on their own, automatically and with full confidence—it's a beautiful thing, great to feel part of."

THE PURPOSEFUL ARCHITECTURE

As I hope you're seeing, repeating the purpose in a variety of contexts bleeds naturally into actually *living* it organizationally, so that individuals within the organization can come to practice it as a discipline, too. The very best way to communicate the Nick's Experience, we find, is not just to broadcast our purpose statement, but to consciously build the Nick's Experience into our operations—to embed it in the actual systems and processes that teammates use every day in performing their jobs. We've developed and adapted a number of tools to make purpose part of everyday life in our restaurants, spanning all the disciplines involved in running a business. These tools include:

- *Operations cards* that break down specific tasks for teammates so that they're done in ways consistent with our purpose.

- *A problem-solving process,* "Issue—Purpose & Values—Solution," which encourages teammates to filter all solutions to a given issue through the prism of our values.
- *Feedback processes* that encourage supervisors to coach in the moment, so that team members understand immediately whether a given behavior is on or off purpose.
- *Moment of Magic cards* that remind team members of specific actions they should follow to cultivate breakthrough, peak experiences in accordance with our purpose.
- *Meditation practices* designed to help teammates clear their minds and focus on living out our purpose in their smallest behaviors.
- *Achievement awards and compensation structures* designed to celebrate performance that is based on our purpose.
- *Architecture and spatial design* that evokes and enables our purpose.
- *Community-based marketing practices* that actualize our purpose, rather than just publicize it.

Most of the tools listed here are inward-facing, operational processes, designed primarily for team members to interface with and use. To further articulate what I mean about working the purpose into operations, I'll focus on the last two outward-facing items on the list, architecture and marketing, as these relate more directly to the task of communicating with the widest possible audience. These two operational articulations of our purpose work in tandem with our purpose statement itself to convey our reason for being to team members and the wider community alike. We'll talk about the other items on the list later on in the book.

Let's first take architecture. In 1994, when I designed our initial restaurant building, I didn't consciously do so with the Nick's Experience in mind, as we hadn't formalized it yet. Still, the building from the very beginning mirrored my personality and my intentions. I knew I wanted to start a family restaurant, and I thought that having the place look rustic was important. Back when I was building houses, I'd collected some old trade magazines, and in one of them I'd seen this really cool, unique barn in California. As I was thinking about what my future restaurant would look like, I remembered that barn and pulled the magazine off the shelf. "Okay," I said, "this is where we're going to start!" I couldn't have anticipated just how spot-on that intuitive choice of a barn was as an articulation of the Nick's Experience, how much it would help our restaurant feel authentic and homey.

I asked my brother Tony, an architect, to help me develop the floor plan. We visited different restaurants to get ideas and assess what worked and what didn't. We didn't want everything on one floor, like a cafeteria, nor did we want concrete floors. We paid a lot of attention to creating something unique that felt a hundred years old—a comfortable, familiar place, like your home. Barns are sometimes too big to really feel intimate, so we solved the problem by incorporating different levels into the floor plan and creating several private seating areas that all look out into the main dining area. Even when people sit in the main dining area, they still feel cozy, as they are surrounded by half walls on either side of the booths.

The main dining area was the core of the restaurant. A huge

fireplace on one wall provided a homey central focal point. We also chose authentic materials as often as we could—for example, constructing the fireplace out of real boulders so it looked old. For the foundation, I went to Chicago and bought truck-loads of granite cobblestones that had been laid down in local streets during the Great Depression. In place of concrete floors, we found hardwood oak, but it was new oak, so I took some big chains and rocks and had fun beating it up to make it look old. For beams and siding, we used material salvaged from an actual barn built in the area in 1870. The beams were hand-hewn, giving the feeling of a very local place—complete with quirks and imperfections—built by our ancestors before they had power tools.

With the floor plan in hand, we considered the lobby and thought, "What first impression do we want to give? What will the guests' experience be from the moment they get out of the car in the parking lot, to when they walk in and wait in the lobby, to when they walk to their table?" To enhance the feeling of "home," my dad suggested building huge doors out of barn beams. We also kept plastic baskets of peanuts on every table so that the shells would fall on the floor and establish a casual environment. We posted pictures of sports teams from the community around our lobby, right where you walk in. We found real antique farm and kitchen tools—actual family heirlooms, not just the reproductions you find in other restaurants—and hung them up on the walls. These were really cool objects: old scooters from the 1950s, children's toy cars, snowshoes and sleds, even an old wooden phone booth.

I could go on and on talking about our real 1920s bar, the old saloon doors, the authentic tin ceiling, the jokes printed on plaques throughout our dining area, the video games in our game room, and the fish tanks that were filled only with the kinds of freshwater fish you'd see in a home aquarium rather than the fancy saltwater fish you see in many restaurants. The point is that we intuitively paid attention to minuscule parts of the design in attempting to realize my internal vision of the restaurant as a homey place for family fun. And because we spent so much time thinking about the small stuff in this way, our restaurants today are naturally aligned with the Nick's Experience, even as our purpose has become much more conscious and explicit.

Pursuing purpose entails risk. Many parts of our design seemed odd to people, starting with the concept of designing a big old barn as a restaurant. My dad thought it would make much more sense to build a generic rectangular building with a mansard roof, since we could rent it out or repurpose it if the restaurant failed. He made similar arguments about other design choices: Wasn't what we were doing more expensive and harder to execute than another option? Sure, from a rational standpoint, we could have done things differently and saved a lot of hassle. With purpose, however, you're tapping into another, more creative part of yourself. In the end, I overcame my nervousness and thought to myself, "If I'm going to do this, I'm going to do it right." That meant pushing the envelope, going the extra mile to get those cobblestones or antiques.

I almost went too far. Halfway through construction, I ran out of money and couldn't get bank financing. So I reached out to friends in the trades and called in favors. I had temporarily gone back to work as a union carpenter to keep my health benefits active in case my restaurant didn't take off. Over eight months, laboring nights and weekends, we built the place. Often I'd start working at 3:30 or 4:00 in the afternoon and continue into the night. The physical space of Nick's was thus both literally and figuratively an outgrowth of what was inside of me—my passion and my purpose. It embodied the sense of community and giving I wanted to project onto the world.

In the restaurant industry, atmosphere matters. When you're inviting people—most of them strangers—into your place for a few hours, you want them to feel comfortable; otherwise they'll never return. No matter what kind of business you're in, it's important to think about how your physical space aligns with and communicates your purpose. How does your physical space relate to your company's reason for being? Does it actively express or contradict it? How did you design your space? If you're the company's founder, did the design emerge from your gut sense of what you were trying to accomplish? What small things can you alter right now to align your space better with your purpose statement? To proceed, think of specific words in the purpose statement and try to connect those with specific elements of your design.

MARKETING FROM THE INSIDE OUT

When establishing a new business, traditional advertising sometimes comes in handy. Billboards, trucks driving around a city, an advertisement in the yellow pages, and the like can help drive recognition. I started out placing ads in brochures for kids' programs—for example, offering coupons for $2 off a pizza—since I thought these meshed well with our brand and value proposition. Eventually I realized that advertising wasn't returning my investment and that it was limiting me to the same brand image other pizza restaurants had. Within a year of working with Rudy and solidifying the company around the Nick's

Experience, we stepped back and said, "Okay, where do we *really* want to spend our money?" We decided to stop all advertising and instead create marketing programs that contributed to the community, since these were more in line with our values. From then on, we'd rely heavily on the *medium* by which we marketed to communicate the message about who we were.

Over the past several years, we've developed and enhanced a number of extremely successful corporate social responsibility programs that, in embodying the Nick's Experience, communicate it better than any advertising could. We have a school incentive program that hands out 18,000 Awesome Achievement Awards to school kids annually; a 10% discount program for teachers; a scholarship program for our team members; a program that provides restaurant tours to youth organizations; a Library Incentive Program that rewards kids for reading; a sponsorship program for local youth sports teams; a program that allows nonprofits to hold fund-raising events in our restaurants and receive 15% of our net profits during the event; and special quarterly benefit events that channel all proceeds from events to needy families and individuals in our community. These and other programs cost us about 5% of net sales but generate a ton of buzz, bring in new guests, and broadcast the spirit of the Nick's Experience in ways that really connect with people. Highlights of the buzz are local and national awards, including being an Illinois finalist for the National Restaurant Association's Restaurant Neighbor Award three times so far, in 2007, 2008, and 2011.

I know these programs work because as I go around talking to guests, I constantly hear, "We've come because we hear a lot about all the ways you give back, and we like the way you do things." Guests approach me all the time and report that they

pass by Applebee's, Red Robin, Buffalo Wild Wings, and Out-
back Steakhouse just down the street to eat and drink with us
because of what we do in the community. They read in the paper
about the benefits we're doing or a family or organizational fund-
raiser event using our restaurant. All this goes to show that a
community and a company can rally together authentically and
for their mutual benefit by acting on and communicating a
purpose.

I also know these programs work because I observe their
effects on our team members. A few years ago, we did a fund-
raiser for Morgan Demming, the daughter of a server who had
suffered severe trauma from a brain aneurysm and been given
little chance of surviving. Without being asked by management,
our team came out in force, wearing pink shirts in honor of Morgan and donating their tips and their time. Members of the community came out, too; the restaurant was packed, with all
proceeds for the day, more than $20,000, going to fund Mor-
gan's expensive care. Everybody involved was affected emotionally, especially our team members. "Oh, I'll never forget it,
seeing people pull together," one of our servers told me. "I've
just never felt anything like that in my life. I worked the lunch
shift and we were so busy, and nobody cared that they were waiting twenty, thirty, forty minutes for a table. The outpouring of
devotion and commitment was just overwhelming. We still talk
about it all the time." When's the last time anybody said anything like that about a TV ad?

Our team members don't merely participate in our marketing efforts; they innovate important new programs to help communicate the Nick's Experience. As one great example, our
recent recession promotions received national recognition in
our industry's leading trade publication, *Nation's Restaurant*

News. During the fall of 2008, as the recession hit our area, our servers noticed that our business was slowing and that fewer families were coming in to eat. Many of our servers themselves had families with kids and husbands who had lost their jobs, so they suffered the bad economy's ravages firsthand. Our servers spotted an opportunity to simultaneously exemplify and broadcast our purpose—especially the part that says "Our dedicated family provides this community . . ."—by allowing hard-hit families a reprieve from the economy one night a week.

On Mondays we offered 50% off in-house orders, and on Tuesdays, 50% off carry-out orders. Business on those two nights, traditionally our slowest, skyrocketed. Not only did we create more jobs for our team and help our bottom line; we also became known as champions of our community. Competing restaurants began copying us, which also helped struggling families. Two years later, as the economy improved, we started to phase out the program, having returned $1.1 million in discounts to our community.

The coolest thing about our approach is that with our team so active, we don't need a marketing department. Despite generating more than $7 million of revenue each year, we employ just one person who is dedicated to "special events and marketing," and she serves essentially to keep things organized. Marketing for us happens organically. It's a cyclical system: By internalizing the Nick's Experience to their core, our team members, old and young, conceive of ideas that further express and communicate our purpose.

Of course, not all of the ideas are great. One recently hired manager was a nice, outgoing guy who interviewed well but did not match the Nick's Experience. Having previously worked for Hooters, he thought we could drive sales by sending our female servers out in bikini tops to do a car wash. That didn't happen, nor do we market ourselves by sponsoring men's softball tournaments. (Ever notice how loud those guys are? Not too family-friendly.) To communicate purpose through marketing, everything you do must be based on the company's purpose. And who better to deliver on that than the very people—our team—who are charged with promoting the Nick's Experience every day.

A final and important thing we do is mobilize social media. Many companies approach tools like Facebook and Twitter with caution, fearful of what team members will do or say online. We find social media a natural fit, since Facebook and Twitter are all about community, and so is our purpose statement. We don't fear what team members might say online because we've spent so much time communicating our purpose that our employees naturally say things that are consistent with it. We do assign one team member to organize and direct our social media efforts, suggesting which topics team members might discuss on their personal Facebook pages during a given week. But then we leave them alone to behave naturally and be themselves as they respond to official Nick's postings and tag us in their own personal postings. Unlike many companies, we don't promulgate guidelines or place any other formal restrictions on what team members do or say.

What defines culture in any organization are actual behaviors—not behaviors desired by executives. Because social media is so transparent, real, and uncontrollable, the culture of your company is going to shine through. When you start with a strong culture built around purpose as the foundation, you can allow social media to be organic. Within just over a year of deploying social media and without much cultivation on our part, we had 5,000 Facebook friends; that speaks directly to the match between what our team does and says and the culture we've built.

VOLCANO ERUPTING

When we first rolled out our purpose statement, we circulated posters around the company that said, "Like a volcano, the 'Nick's Purpose' was always there but was lying dormant for seven years. Now it's erupted and it's time to *live it*!" And live it we have. Purpose can't just be some lofty, unattainable thing floating on the surface of your culture. It's got to be as tangible as the thick old barn beams that support our roof and the steaming hot pizza we serve at community events inside our restaurant. That's how you move from the head to the heart in connecting with team members. That's how you create a work environment that's meaningful to people and worth being part of.

So many companies genuinely want to make a difference in the world, and many of them do succeed, yet often people forget that all change starts with the individual. It's great to donate money to an African charity or write a check to the American Cancer Society. But I believe real progress comes from paying attention to the individual's performance within the context of the stated company purpose (assuming that that purpose is legitimate and in service of the greater good). It comes from paying attention to life *inside* the company, all the way down to the most menial, entry-level members of the team. Because only when you align with and deliver against the culture in big and small ways does the spirit of your company truly come alive. The next chapter will begin to cover some of our inward-facing

tools, processes, and tactics in the course of introducing a critical principle for any purpose-driven company: Encourage your
team members to be themselves. As we'll see, if you trust your
people to behave spontaneously on the job, they'll reward you by
drawing the company's purpose out from the one place that
really matters, their hearts.

CHAPTER THREE
Let People Be Themselves

Just as companies need to focus inwardly on operations when seeking to actualize purpose, so, too, must they attend to the intrinsic motivations and psychology of individuals. The psychologist Abraham Maslow expressed the importance of intrinsic motivations in his hierarchy of needs, which examines the various desires and motivations behind human development. Maslow placed personal fulfillment and related notions of creativity, meaning, and individual expression at the top of his hierarchy, above the most basic needs like food, water, safety, love, and the respect of others. Only when people feel comfortable being who they are will they be truly satisfied, and it goes without saying that leaders and organizations that can help people achieve this fulfillment will inspire great things.

Culture comes to life most completely when team members elicit your company's purpose on their own terms and in their own ways, as a form of self-expression. That's not going to happen in a command-and-control environment in which the company dictates everything employees do and trains them to behave like everyone else. On the contrary, the best way to ensure that your team members join in your high-performance culture is to let them be themselves.

The quirky, casual feel of our restaurants signals to team members that it's okay to behave in unscripted, spontaneous ways at work, and although we take extreme care in correcting behavior that goes counter to our purpose, we never cast judgment on individuals and their tastes. We also trust our team members to resolve conflicts on their own, teaching them how to create an environment in which everyone can talk without feeling belittled or resentful. When we train new employees, we show them how to perform a task correctly and explain how they might make the process their own. In our hiring process, we also screen to ensure that our values align with those of our new hires—something that lets us feel comfortable trusting diverse team members to be themselves.

It might seem that we're sowing chaos in our workplaces, but we've found that spontaneous, unpredictable, unscripted behavior, far from disrupting our operations, enables our team to outperform expectations and arrive at solutions we never dreamed of. That's because we're allowing an individual's genius to emerge in its own way. If we don't open the door to unscripted behavior, even behavior I personally wouldn't adopt, everybody's performance merely conforms to the level of our best manager rather than being the best it can be for each employee individually. Are the good sports teams those with a lone superstar or those where everybody else is *made better* by the superstar? Unscripted behavior creates a high-performance culture by leveraging the entire team's talents in support of the overall purpose. In letting go of some control—the "trust" part of Trust and Track—you unleash your workforce's natural passion and allow great things to happen.

GEORGIE

When it comes to our servers, unscripted behavior can mean many things: a full-bellied laugh; remembering guests' names and details about their lives; telling jokes; using certain facial expressions; inquiring in a natural, genuine way about how a guest is feeling; asking more specific questions instead of the usual "What can I get you?"; saying something friendly like "Have some peanuts" when walking away from a table; asking specific questions about guest satisfaction instead of just "How is everything?"; taking time to chat during the meal; showing a sense of urgency in bringing the guest the check when they wish to leave; using the guest's name and saying a special good-bye instead of just walking away with the check. In short, unscripted behavior makes the difference between a generic, uninspired table experience and one that is fun, memorable, truly extraordinary—and in full alignment with the Nick's Experience.

We've had many outstanding servers at Nick's, but none stands out in my mind as strongly as Georgie. She was a short, stocky Italian-American woman in her thirties, a brunette version of Laverne on the *Laverne & Shirley* TV show. You knew immediately when she was in the house because you could hear her laughter and her friendly, high-pitched voice clear across the room. Visually, she stuck out, too, with no fewer than thirteen earrings in her ears, a comparable number of rings on her fingers, and tattoos.

Most companies probably wouldn't accommodate a team member as spirited and expressive as Georgie. They'd regard her as a threat, a force to be contained. We viewed her as a force we could harness in support of the Nick's Experience. As mentioned, we train our servers to greet everyone who comes within five steps; Georgie had so much positive energy that she naturally greeted everyone she saw within twenty steps. She sang and danced as she shuttled between the Heart of House (our name for the kitchen) and the tables. Guests and other team members couldn't help but be themselves because they saw Georgie doing just that so colorfully, so idiosyncratically, and so happily. Her laughter and good cheer infected everyone.

Perhaps the best indication that Georgie's unscripted behavior advanced the Nick's Experience was the incredibly close bonds she formed with our guests. Back in 2003, a man and a woman used to visit our Crystal Lake restaurant every Friday night. Each was going through a tough divorce, and they would stop by Nick's for a meal after attending group therapy sessions together. Georgie served them a number of times, and soon they began requesting her. They liked how she joked with them, took time to chat, and shared her own stories around relationships and divorce. One night, after about eight months of weekly visits, the couple got engaged at one of Georgie's tables. Whether Georgie had anything to do with that, I don't know, but I do know that the couple came in one night a few years later and presented Georgie with five $100 bills taped to a card, as well as a vest depicting people dancing, since, according to Georgie, "when they would watch me serve, they said I had this rhythm, my own unique dance." The couple has since married and moved to North Carolina, and they still send Georgie Christmas cards. Years later, Georgie has left our company to run her own catering business, but she is still beside herself. "I mean, in my lifetime, I never thought what I did, I mean just serving tables and stuff like that, just doing my own crazy thing, would mean so much to people. But that's what happened."

ACTIVATING FLOW

I don't have a college education, but I'm always reading books and articles about business and personal development, and I've found that scholars and consultants have a pretty good idea about how Georgie's freedom to be herself yields higher performance. Basically, we gave her an opportunity to experience "flow," a psychological state that one writer has described as "literally the awake-dreaming state of mind" that happens when you can "move through the space of a problem, holding many design 'moves' in the mind at once, and suspending self-criticism while retaining idea-based judgment."* When I think about Georgie weaving among tables on a busy Friday night, somehow handling requests from three groups of guests, checking on her orders in the Heart of House, greeting everyone in sight, singing, dancing, laughing—well, that embodies creative flow as well as anything. She was somehow able to navigate a pretty demanding and complex work environment, not only getting everything right, but pleasing our guests and delivering the Nick's Experience to the highest degree, because she was able to be herself and behave in ways that felt natural.

When individuals feel free to suspend self-criticism and experience flow, the team they form can experience collective flow. One of our servers uses that term to describe the smooth working of our teams, especially on busy, stressful nights. "Everybody just works so well together, and there's such great teamwork. And everybody just excels, there's just a flow, a really

....

* Jon Kolko, "Cultural Values That Will Make Your Office an Idea Factory," www .fastcodesign.com, January 19, 2011. I also recommend reading Mihaly Csikszentmihalyi's classic book *Flow* (1990).

good flow between coworkers. And whether it's from the Front of House or the Heart of House, I think the guests really see that and appreciate that. They just enjoy being there to observe us." Group flow is like a jazz quartet that locks in on a riff or members of a basketball squad that pass the ball almost effortlessly and win the game at the very last second. Group flow at Nick's occurs when our Heart of House churns out dozens of pizzas within a few short minutes to meet the dinnertime rush, even handling complex special orders. It occurs when a blinding Chicago snowstorm hits and a bunch of team members spontaneously pick up shovels to clear our sidewalks, keeping our dining room operating normally all along. It's pure magic, something wonderful to experience and behold.

Flow leads to a positive collective experience, but that doesn't mean it manifests itself in the same way for everyone. At Nick's, flow has many faces: Steph, who rolls dough for us in our Heart of House, senses that the team's energy level is flagging. On her own initiative, she uses her imagination to help her coworkers invent fun contests and games to get things moving again. Dan, another Heart of House team member, makes a new team member, Kevin, feel accepted by purposely including him in conversations—again, on his own initiative—and giving Kevin a pat on the back after he finished training in a particular task. Joe, a pizza maker, ventures into the dining room to get a drink. A little kid comes up and says hi. Joe asks the kid his name and spends several minutes making conversation. In each of these cases, team members didn't evince an especially colorful or unorthodox personality, as Georgie did, but they still let their personalities out in small ways that enhanced our performance, made the workplace more pleasant, and forged bonds between people.

Often team members' unique talents bring about special results for us. Brittany, a nineteen-year-old drama major who has worked for us part-time for about three years, loves to sing and is very good at it. When she answers our phones in carry-out, she sounds like she is singing, "Thank you for calling Nick's Pizza & Pub." At our host desk, she lights up the lobby with her high-energy welcomes, breaking into song during slow moments and then going right back to work as volume picks up. She is so good at this that about two months ago, she rewrote a page in our training manual on how to work the host's microphone, describing how to have fun on the microphone with voice inflection and how to call a guest up to the host desk in an entertaining way. We know guests enjoy this because we often see them doubled over in laughter. Other team members laugh along and help Brittany ad-lib; it becomes a mini improv session right there in our restaurant.

Ellen, a fireplug with a huge smile, is a mom extraordinaire who knows how to read people and understand what they want. Standing only five feet tall, she has six kids, each under the age of seven, including a set of triplets. She typically only works dinners and often closes the restaurant so as to make some extra money while her kids are sleeping. I don't know how she does it, but she has enough energy for three people. Her spontaneity and sense of humor allow her to forge instantaneous connections with our guests. She bounds up to a table, ponytail bouncing, greeting families with small children by remarking on what the kids are wearing, suggesting kid-friendly drinks, making animal sounds. She chats with guests about a movie they've seen or notices the names guests call each other. She'll say, "My daughter's name is Maggie" or "I have a friend named Sam." Sometimes other servers call upon her to help handle difficult situations in her unique way because she's so good at relating to people. Recently, when a somewhat intoxicated guest grabbed at the elbow of a young female server, Ellen came over and in a friendly, joking manner said, "Hey, take it easy, Tyson." It was just the right comment to defuse the situation without causing offense to anyone (except perhaps Mike Tyson).

Then there's our server Susan. In 2005 she was taking care of guests at an end-of-year banquet for a soccer team. After everyone from the party had left, the coach, a middle-aged man, was sitting alone in the room, reading thank-you cards his team had left for him. His eyes were glistening with tears. Although Susan was busy with chores, she decided to sit and chat with him.

"You know," he said, pointing to the cards. "This is why I do it. For the kids. I'm just so overwhelmed to know that my coaching them means so much to them. The crazy thing is, it's *me* who should be saying thank you to *them*. I feel so grateful!"

"I know just what you mean," Susan said, "because that's how I feel working at Nick's. It's about the team, about the sense of community you feel, the chance to give back and take care of people."

"It really makes you feel good, doesn't it," the man said. "At the end of the day, you know it's all worth it."

"Absolutely," Susan said.

The conversation went on like this for five or ten minutes, and the man was touched by what Susan was saying. He went to the bar and had a couple of drinks, watching her go about her work. On his way out, he handed her the check and said, "Thank you very much. Really, you did a great job with the banquet, and I really enjoyed talking to you." On her way to the register, Susan happened to glance down at the man's credit card slip. She couldn't believe her eyes: He'd given her a $1,000 tip.

Thinking it was a mistake, she ran out to see if she could catch him in the parking lot. He was just getting into his truck. "Excuse me!" Susan called. "I think this is wrong! You tipped—"

He smiled. "No, it's right. I want you to take that, I want you to enjoy it. I appreciate what you do and how you took time out to listen to me talk about the kids and everything."

Susan burst out crying and gave him a hug. "It was totally out of the blue," she remembers. "I mean, I never in a million years ever expected anything like that. Of course, I was thrilled to receive a $1,000 tip, and at the same time, I was just like, wow, now I know what my purpose is here. This is what we do here, you know? I was just really touched. I was astounded."

As Susan's story illustrates, unscripted behavior on the part of teammates can and does lead to some really special behavior on the part of guests. Reflecting on her ability to be herself on the job and on the culture at Nick's, Susan adds, "It's amazing, how no matter what I seem to have going on in my personal life or how I just sometimes don't feel like going to work, when I walk into the restaurant, I feel alive. We hear a lot from guests that it seems like we're having so much fun. And we are. It's not fake, it's not pretend, it's not forced or anything. It's authentic, true fun. I think they can really feel it, they experience it, they see it, and they become freer too."

THE LIMITS OF INTRINSIC MOTIVATION

Opportunities for self-expression and intrinsic motivation aren't the only things required to develop a high-performance team. Good, old-fashioned extrinsic motivations like money and promotions matter, too. In his book *Drive*, Daniel Pink argues that a carrot-and-stick approach might have worked better during the industrial age, when many tasks were mechanical and rote, and the goal was to improve how fast you did something. In the twenty-first century, however, much of what people do at work is creative, so they need the things we're talking about here—autonomy, mastery, and purpose—to perform at their absolute best. The interesting thing about a pizza restaurant, and I suspect many businesses today, is that the more mechanistic, industrial-age style of work is still partially in vogue. Work performed by our servers, hosts, bartenders, and others might involve a lot of creativity, but in the kitchen our people are putting together pizzas on what amounts, at least in part, to an assembly line, and speed does matter.

I introduced my Operating Partner Scott to Pink's ideas, and we thought we'd try a social-science experiment to see which kind of motivation worked best in which environment. We tried out extrinsic motivation one Tuesday night. It was Takeout Tuesday, a half-price pizza night, which meant we couldn't churn out the pizzas fast enough to meet demand. With twenty-six people crammed into our 1,500-square-foot Heart of House, and with temperatures there exceeding 100 degrees, we needed the team to crank up the volume without sacrificing quality. Scott's idea: Offer $20 to the pizza maker who made the most pizzas. It was the perfect carrot-and-stick reward model. We could count on quality because we routinely assigned a pizza checker to stand at the end of the line and double-check for mistakes or any slight quality variations. So what happened? Record sales and no mistakes. No need for anything special that would spark creativity or self-expression on the part of our team. Just a simple monetary incentive.

This is not to say we don't see intrinsic motivation and creativity in our Heart of House. James, one of our team members, loves coming up with new ideas for our menu. I took his suggestion that we offer grilled-chicken calzones, and it has remained a popular menu item for years. Recently he proposed we offer a double-decker breakfast pizza with eggs; we don't serve breakfast, so I'm not sure that will fly, but I loved his creativity. Members of our Heart of House also express themselves by making spontaneous process refinements. Esau, one of our pizza makers, described his own unique secret for making pizzas fast: "When we're in the back making sausage pizza and we need to step it up, I'll tell people to imagine that each piece of sausage you put on represents $1 million or a life you're saving—you naturally want to put on as many as possible in the allotted time."

Recognizing that internal motivations play a role in the Heart of House, we try to let them come to the surface seamlessly. When the dinner rush is over and the winner gets his or her $20 bill, the Heart of House team goes off as individuals to break down and clean the whole facility. We don't supervise their every move or dictate to them exactly how to do it. They get to exercise creativity in this part of their jobs too, and we encourage individuality and self-expression in them as we do with everyone at Nick's. Now, can taking out the trash really be creative? Just ask seventeen-year-old Esau. He's devised his own method of removing boxes by stacking them on a dolly and strapping them in using a spare apron. Other team members will leave their stations in the kitchen stocked at the end of a shift—a helpful behavior and not one mandated or described on our operations cards. Because we celebrate such small, seemingly insignificant creative opportunities when they occur, our Heart of House teams tend to leave at the end of the night tired, but not beaten down. They feel a sense of accomplishment, and they look forward to returning for their next shift because they get a chance to add their own value to even rote tasks, serving a purpose above and beyond an extra $20. As one of our Heart of House team members, Joe Delucca, tells me, "Man, I love it when it gets busy. Yeah, it's hot and it's chaos, and we never knew how we're going to make it through, but somehow we do, and everybody gets the job done in their own special way. At the end of the night, we know we've kicked ass!"

Scott and I wondered if external or intrinsic motivations would work better on our Front of House staff, the people with more creative jobs. We asked our servers, hosts, and bartenders what kind of monetary incentive we could dangle that would get them to work harder. They couldn't give us an answer, which made sense. For them, simply going faster wouldn't earn them more money. Quite the opposite: They'd make more mistakes, provide poorer service, and probably end up earning less in tips. So what we did instead was post a "server's score card" in our break area that reported the average guest check amount for each server. In effect, we created a competition to see whose could increase the most over a four-week period. This would trigger intrinsic motivation and unscripted behavior that was based on our purpose: Team members would have a chance to see how creative they could get in serving guests, so that guests would enjoy their experience even more, perhaps stay for dessert—and, of course, leave bigger tips.

Within that four-week period, servers began to ask more open-ended questions when suggesting appetizers. They used descriptive words to describe products more effectively. They hustled more to provide prompter service. Guess what? The average guest-check amount increased from $10.70 to $11.50. Since between 900 and 1,200 guests come through our doors on most busy weekend lunch and dinner shifts, that means an increase of approximately $800 in sales. To me, this is proof positive that unscripted behavior really does work, especially in situations where creativity is a big part of the job.

NEVER PUNISH PEOPLE FOR BEING THEMSELVES

To encourage self-expression, we do many things, whether it's a manager giving a thumbs-up to a team member who has just engaged in unscripted behavior based on our purpose or a profile of one of our employees in our quarterly internal newsletter. But is it really possible for a company to make room for spontaneous, natural expression in all its forms without feeling nervous about what team members might do?

So far in this chapter, we've been talking about the "trust" part of Trust and Track, but the "track" part is vital too. Even as we give people permission to be themselves, we scrutinize our teams to make sure they stay focused on our purpose in their self-expression. A young waiter following in my dad's footsteps might like to use, well, colorful language in his casual conversations with others, but while this might promote collegiality with his friends outside of work, it doesn't fit our family-friendly atmosphere. Our managers are highly trained to spot such off-purpose behavior and to coach and mentor individuals in the moment on how to correct it. We also have a well-developed system for delivering ongoing formal feedback to team members irrespective of their experience level. I'll describe this in more detail in Chapter Six, but for now I'll make one key point: Our systems are designed to catch and correct off-purpose behavior without ever punishing people for being themselves.

When someone like Georgie shows up, we don't tell her to

calm down or tone it down. Any coaching we do is limited to the task itself, not the personality of the individual who is performing it. When someone happens to violate our purpose—say, by wearing a too-short dress at the host's desk—we coach her by going back to our values and asking her how what she's doing might be in line with the values. "What kind of dress *is* appropriate? Would your grandma approve of you wearing that? Why or why not? Was there a question in your mind when you put that on in the morning? What do you think? Let's analyze this together." We help the team member understand "why," and as a result we find that the offending behavior seldom reoccurs (young people today really value a collaborative, coaching approach to management as opposed to a top-down, dictatorial style). If the violation is glaring, we ask the person to go home, change, and come back. But we don't frown on them, give them the silent treatment, mock them, make sarcastic comments, or treat them in some other disrespectful way.

We take special care when dealing with young team members who are new to the workforce. Some people who work for us are as young as sixteen; their egos are often fragile, and they are tentative, feeling their way around the workplace, experimenting, seeking a voice and persona for themselves. When they come out of their shells in even the slightest way, we encourage every word—especially if their ideas are incorrect or ineffective. The important thing, we feel, is that they speak up and put themselves on the line. Simply saying, "Great, thanks so much for contributing, glad to see you're thinking of ways we can improve" does so much to encourage their growth process so that in the future, when they *do* have solid ideas, they won't be afraid to put them forward.

As humans, we naturally tend to avoid delicate situations

and let small violations pass. That's dangerous, because over time ignoring even small problems can lead to erosion of the culture. As we tell team members, step into conflict. If a team member is not doing her job or if she's showing disrespect for another team member, don't just watch her do it over and over; say something right then, in the moment. But say the right thing. Don't make too big of a deal about a violation. Don't be dramatic. Don't exaggerate by saying, "Everybody's always late" or "Those hosts are always wearing short skirts" when in fact only one or two people did it once or twice. Make the intervention quick, urgent, to the point. Speak to the data, and take all drama out of it. Offer coaching, and be sure to pose open-ended questions (for example, "Tell me about the choice to wear jeans that have holes in them today." "What does it say in the team member handbook about uniforms?" "Can you find a way of getting the proper uniform today?"). Using these guidelines, we can turn everyday errors into valuable learning opportunities that strengthen understanding of what our company is all about.

WRITE UNSCRIPTED BEHAVIOR INTO JOB DESCRIPTIONS

Another critically important reason we can allow for unscripted behavior without fear is that we make it explicitly part of every job. Guided by our consultant Rudy Miick, we've developed extensive definitions that clearly specify what we call the "art" and "science" of team-member roles. The "science" part includes the objective tasks or actions the team member must perform to make sure the job is done right, while the "art" part comprises the more subjective elements of the task—the places where different individuals can diverge in how they get the job done. We've gone to great lengths to define excellence, so we emphasize the need to get both the "art" and the "science" right. But the "art" side allows each team member to inject his or her own spirit into even the most mundane or rote tasks.

Written into all team member job descriptions are a number of elements, mentioned earlier, that we think contribute to what we call Moments of Magic in our restaurants: greeting everyone within five steps of you, greeting all guests coming into and out of the restaurants, answering the phones correctly, teamwork, and the Grandma Test (that is, would your grandma approve of your behavior?). Each of these, in turn, is broken down into "art" and "science." The science of answering the phones is to do so within three rings, say "Nick's Pizza & Pub" and the location, give your name and the time of day, and communicate an action step (for example, "How can I help you?"). But we also specify areas of artfulness in which individuals can shine through: tone of voice, the energy employed as they answer the phone, the awareness they maintain of what the other person is saying, etc. Likewise, with our five-step greetings, the science is making verbal or nonverbal contact and connecting with guests. How team members do it—how they anticipate the contact, how they scan the room, the gracefulness and flow with which they behave—is up to them.

Let's say you want to train as a pizza maker in our Heart of House. Aside from teaching you the basic behaviors all team members practice, our training manual breaks that specific job down for you into a series of components, including safety and sanitation, washing silverware and pie servers, the handling of knives, stocking and storage, flattening dough, labeling the pizza boxes, cutting the dough, taking care of the ingredients, managing time on the job properly, etc. In our training packet for this position, we break down each of these into "art" and "science."

The science of caring for the pizza ingredients includes things like making sure the quality is up to par, that all the available toppings are there, that they are prepared to spec, and that the ingredient bins are fully stocked. Yet we also clearly articulate areas where team members can exercise individual judgment—how they use their various senses to evaluate the ingredients, how they go about keeping the bins fully stocked. Below is a more specific list of how we break down the art and science of our ingredients process.

INGREDIENTS

Art	Science
Smell	Food quality
Touch	Rotation—FIFO
Eyes	Day dots
Taste	Knowledge of all available toppings
Constant awareness	Toppings prepped to spec
Fully stocked	Fully stocked
Nick's Experience	Reporting waste

Similarly, when we train executives and floor managers in performing white-collar tasks, we also specify both the "art" and the "science" of the activity. With the delegation of work, for instance, managers are expected to be specific in their instructions, define what success in the delegated task looks like, tie the task to some larger rationale, give clear deadlines, and so on. We even have a flowchart that maps out general guidelines for when, under what circumstances, and to whom managers should delegate. Beyond that, though, we recognize that much of delegation is an "art" that individuals will do in their own, unscripted ways. As we tell our managers, they can express themselves in such things as the way they serve as mentors and allies, the way they develop a coaching rapport, and the actual language they use to convey our purpose and values to the team member while delegating the task.

Defining roles to allow for unscripted behavior comprises a clear departure from command and control. We're specifically limiting how much we dictate to team members and *trusting* them with at least a portion of their jobs. At the same time, we're establishing clear standards in the vital "science" portions, defining excellence in the metrics we use for each and every job function. This system amounts to a pretty stringent discipline, on both the "art" and "science" sides. It's not easy greeting a guest or taking an order in exactly the right way, even if you determine portions of that task. We're allowing flexibility for individuality, but we're also asking team members to exercise mindfulness to make sure they stay as close as possible to the purpose. Employees must dedicate a great deal of energy, time, attention, and patience over a period of time to get the art side of their jobs right. If anything, we think our art and science system is *more* stringent than typical training approaches that don't specifically outline areas for people to improvise on their own.

THE ROLE OF HIRING FOR VALUES

A critical system that we've put in place to assure that unscripted behavior lines up with purpose is our hiring protocol. We feel comfortable trusting team members to express themselves because we take so much care at the outset to assure alignment of their values and personalities with the Nick's Experience. I hear a lot about companies "hiring for attitude" instead of task management, on the grounds that it's far easier to teach people specific tasks than it is to get their personality to fit in with your culture. In the most general sense, that's what we do; we hire for values alignment and synergy.

Our hiring process begins when we put our purpose and values statements on the cover sheet of our application and ask applicants to evaluate whether these really resonate with them. After filling out an application, the applicant hands it to a manager or trainer who is well versed in interviewing skills, including how to track body language, tone of voice, and language. During a two- or three-minute conversation, our team member evaluates whether the applicant is the kind of high-energy, outgoing, gregarious, and respectful person we're seeking. He or she also asks questions designed to see if applicants are just looking for a job or are attracted to Nick's because of the Nick's Experience. If the team member accepting the application decides in that first minute or two that a fit doesn't exist, he'll thank the applicant and let her go. Otherwise, he'll take her over to an interview binder and schedule an interview for another day.

In the interview itself, applicants fill out a personality survey called the Predictive Index, which we find simpler and more effective than other psychological profiling tools, such as Myers-Briggs.* We also ask applicants to write out answers to eight open-ended questions, such as "Describe yourself in one word"; "What would you do if you saw someone stealing?";

....

* See http://www.piworldwide.com/Products/Predictive-Index-System.aspx.

"Why should we hire you?"; and so on. These questions emphasize real rather than hypothetical experiences; we want to see
how people behave in the moment, and we inquire closely into
how they behaved in certain other work situations—for example,
"Give me an example of when you got slammed with four tables
all at once. What are the first and second things you did in that
situation?" "Tell me about a time you were in a job situation and
had to choose between a friendship and what you believed to be
the right thing to do." "How did 'fun' show up for you in your
last job?"

After the paperwork is done, a pair of our trained
interviewers—managers or trainers rather than dedicated
human-resource staff—talk through these questions with applicants. They also ask interviewees to do one of several exercises
or activities. They specifically avoid using the word "role-play,"
since we strive to create authenticity and real situations in the
interview, and "role-play" suggests that the interaction will
somehow not be real. For those applying to work as a team member in the Heart of House, we're interested in seeing how fast
they can move, so we ask them to take a lap through the restaurant, find three things they'd improve if it was their restaurant,
and tell us what they are. Then, in order to gauge whether their
notion of speed matches our own, we'll ask them to rate on a
scale from 1 to 5 the speed at which they were moving during
that lap. In all our questioning and tests, we're thinking about
our ideal level of A+ performance and assessing whether the
interviewee's assessment of A+ performance matches it.

Influenced by Malcolm Gladwell's book *Blink*, which
explores the human tendency to make quick, gut judgments in
daily life, we keep the interview short, about fifteen minutes, so

our interviewers walk away with a gut impression of an applicant. But these are fifteen pretty intense minutes. All along, our interviewers are tracking many dimensions of behavior. Do applicants' faces redden under tough questioning? Do they maintain their train of thought? Do they do more talking or giggling? During the fifteen minutes, we don't let the interviewee ask us any questions. This keeps us on track and maintains the interview's validity as an experiment, since letting applicants ask questions gives them a chance to regain control and lessen the stress of the situation.

When the person gets up and leaves the interview, the two interviewers decide if he or she has passed or not. Both have to issue a resounding "yes"; we treat a "maybe" from either one as a "no." If both people did like the applicant, we schedule a second interview, which likewise consists of an exercise and questions. One interviewer will be the same as in the previous sessions, one different; the person who has already seen the applicant can track consistency, while the person who hasn't adds a fresh perspective. To be hired at Nick's, you have to receive five yes votes from four people on three different days.

Does this seem extreme? It's true, we're not interviewing experienced hires for a job carrying a six-figure paycheck. We're a pizza restaurant interviewing sixteen-year-olds for a job that pays not much more than minimum wage. Yet we're hell-bent on assuring a clear fit between purpose and values and our potential hires. We select people whose natural behavior we believe is likely to align well with the Nick's Experience and, further, who seem genuinely interested in and capable of joining a learning organization built around a purpose. All this work up front makes possible our Trust and Track approach and, specifically, our openness to unscripted behavior.

LEARNING TO LOOSEN UP

This chapter has outlined the benefits of unscripted behavior as well as some of the practical tools that bring our broader Trust and Track approach to life. We've seen that unscripted behavior, far from bringing chaos to the workplace, can boost the performance of entire teams to unforeseen heights. Yet the organization has to open itself to the genius of individual teammates—clear space for it, nurture it, celebrate it, protect it. This means maintaining standards of excellence rooted in our purpose but putting increased responsibility on the shoulders of team members to meet those standards in their own idiosyncratic ways.

You might come away from this chapter thinking, "Man, allowing for unscripted behavior is a ton of work." You're right! We can trust team members to express themselves only because we're so deliberate as an organization about how we define tasks, hire, train, and track on-the-job performance. We're hiring and training people to become devotees to our purpose, but that means that we have to be devotees, too.

Fostering unscripted behavior is hard for other reasons. As leader, I have to accept that people will diverge from my preconceived notions of how to perform particular jobs. Just the other day, two of our hosts developed an impromptu comedy show while fooling around on the microphone. Not quite what I had in mind, but hey, it wasn't off purpose, so how could I shut it down? We also have servers who have become good friends with older couples who frequent our restaurants, so much so that they pay visits to these guests in their homes. That, too, would feel strange to someone like me, since I am more private. But again, accepting that discomfort is part of the challenge of inviting people to be themselves.

The more general challenge is giving up an ego-based need for control—my ingrained identity as the Fearless Leader. Letting people be themselves on the job means allowing them influence in defining the look and feel of a culture. It means allowing them a *leadership* role in the management of day-to-day affairs and stepping aside to the greatest extent possible. I might have started Nick's, but that doesn't mean I can or should dictate every last thing about it. It also doesn't mean I've figured out every last detail about how best to run my business. If our team's performance is better because I've given up a little bit of control, and because we have boisterous, quirky people like Georgie walking around, then that's just great!

Our approach doesn't stop at unscripted behavior, either. We take leadership from below so seriously that we invest considerable resources in training even the least-experienced team members to behave proactively on behalf of our purpose. How we do that—and the incredible results we realize—is the subject of the next chapter.

CHAPTER FOUR
Train Team Members to Lead

Many organizations offer leadership programs to top recruits to help them advance. But what about everyone else? A high-performance culture requires that *everyone* lead, even and especially when managers aren't around. Team members, not managers, drive the business, and unanticipated energy from the grassroots level can actually push managers to new heights, inspiring them to work harder rather than just delegate from the top down.

A big reason we tap the energies of people like Georgie is that we treat even pimply-faced sixteen-year-old dishwashers as genuine leaders in the making. We hire people with leadership potential, invite them to behave proactively during orientation, and design our workplace experience as a dynamic incubation zone for self-motivated action. Because we expect all team members to actively further the Nick's Experience and their own growth, we engage and energize them in a way top-down organizations can't.

At the heart of our emphasis on leadership is our extensive training program. We teach sixteen- and seventeen-year-olds the sophisticated communications, coaching, and conflict-management skills any leader needs. (As I describe in Chapter

Seven, we teach them financial skills, too.) We also give team-mates a paradigm for solving day-to-day issues themselves, without managers, in ways that align with our culture. Even as we encourage our hires to have fun, they learn on the job to become observant of their own behavior, so that they can contribute to our culture minute-to-minute and in any situation. In this way, the restaurant serves as a school, a community of individuals working hard to better incorporate the tools and enhance our culture while still retaining space to express their individuality.

Many of our youngest team members, who arrive with little to no work experience, step right up into leadership positions in other companies they eventually join. That's because we have seventeen-year-olds training forty-year-old executives on kitchen tasks and twenty-one-year-olds leading forty-year-old servers and bartenders through a high-volume $10,000 shift. Can you imagine the confidence these experiences instill? Empowering everyone to lead also helps the company's bottom line. We don't pay outside companies to innovate new products and processes; our team does that. And the more our people strive on their own to develop themselves and pursue our purpose, the more we can trust them and the less we need to rely on managers to police everything. Helping team members develop into leaders underpins the entire Trust and Track paradigm. A business in which everybody is taught and encouraged to lead is simply a higher-performance business, in addition to being a more pleasant, vibrant, and exciting place to work.

HIRING, TRAINING, AND RETAINING EMERGING LEADERS

Remember those intense interviews described in the last chapter? Besides relying on them to screen for compatibility, we use them to determine an individual's innate capacity to show initiative, step up in stressful situations, and inspire others. When scheduling an initial interview, we don't assign prospective team members an interview time but require that they pick a date and time on their own from a list of available slots. At the interview itself, we then ask open-ended questions that yield deeper insights into a person's character. We might say, "Give me one example of how, when you've been a part of a team or a group, you took the performance of that team to the next level" or "When you have had scheduling conflicts, how did you manage them? How did you handle that for yourself?" Knowing that many of our recruits have never worked before, we ask about their everyday lives to find answers to these not-so-easy questions. How do they behave during basketball practice when the coach isn't there? Do they offer on their own initiative to help younger teammates? Do they volunteer to do the grunt work everybody else declines?

Our hiring process seeks out a certain kind of leader—individuals who can jump in and collaborate as part of a team, people who enjoy sacrificing for the sake of a communal good, who gain satisfaction from raising up those around them, and who take charge of their own growth. We want people who will become not only great managers, but supportive mentors like Phil Jackson, Howard Schultz, and Jack Welch. When we gaze across the interviewing table, whether it's at a sixteen–year-old who wants to be a hostess or at a thirty-seven-year-old interested in being a front-line manager, we don't care about their experience or how much revenue we think they could bring in on their own. We're trying to determine whether others naturally gravitate toward this person, not because of what he may be shouting in an attempt to garner respect but just because of who he is.

No system is perfect, and people sometimes make it into Nick's who aren't intrinsically motivated or who subscribe to the old command-and-control mentality. That's where our intense orientation process kicks in. New teammates receive their own training folders at the beginning of each shift and are expected to keep track of them. They're expected to schedule training sessions for themselves and show up at designated times. They're introduced to our leadership training, which I'll describe in a minute, as well as to our system of operations cards, which specify tasks to be performed in both their "art" and "science" components without direct managerial supervision. After every training shift, they engage in a Feedback Loop with managers during which they're asked to define what they did well during the shift and what they need to improve (see Chapter Six for more detail on the Feedback Loop). Recruits who expect others to tell them what to do or who watch the clock quickly realize they're in way over their heads. They feel like outsiders, and most of the time, they leave within thirty days.

Our system of skills training, to which new hires are exposed from the first day, both instills a sense of responsibility and rewards those who act on their own initiative. All new, entry-level hires learn how to make pizzas in our kitchen no matter what position we hired them for, and they also train for their position. Once they master skills for that position, they control how much they earn and how rapidly they ascend by signing up for and completing training classes in other positions. These "201 classes," as we call them, allow team members to become "certified" in skill areas such as host, server, bartender, dishwasher, and the like.

Certify in three positions, and we give you a tan hat to wear and call you a "rookie." Six positions makes you a red hat, or a "pro." Mastering nine positions makes you an "expert," and you get to wear a black hat. You earn more as you acquire more skills—not because you've worked with us for a given length of time or because a manager thinks you deserve it. Since education is the only path for advancement, team members know they're in charge of their own training and come to *us* asking for it. Those who don't ask find themselves languishing behind their peers and tend to find their way to the door on their own before too long.

The "onboarding" task here isn't simply to train emerging leaders and weed out those who slip through the cracks; it's to *retain* bright, proactive, self-motivated individuals and keep them interested. Many people in the human-resources field talk about employee "engagement" as a top priority of a company, but I've found that the most effective way to keep team

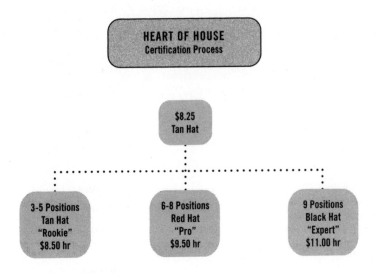

members engaged is to aim higher and build a system of employee enrichment. When you have systems in place that allow people to develop and to emerge as leaders, they will naturally feel engaged with their work.*

In most companies, participation in a training program hinges on your formal review and requires approval by a higher-up. We require no formal approval for certification in skills. At every stage, we let people know that we are grooming them to be leaders in their own lives and also to lead and inspire those around them; that as a company, our goal is not to tell them what to do or how to behave, but simply to help people feel accepted, supported, and successful (in other words, enriched).

One person might complete the host training in a year, another in three months, but in the end their success depends on their performance during training, which is quantitatively rated. Age doesn't matter, which is why we have eighteen-year-olds with many certifications training novice forty-year-olds. Our certification program provides a clear map for anybody who wants to climb the ladder by acquiring more skills. As team members progress in a way that feels natural and authentic to them, they come to feel more and more accountable for their own success, they discover the deep satisfaction that comes from mastering skills, and they feel increasingly empowered to contribute proactively to the Nick's Experience. They also feel stronger

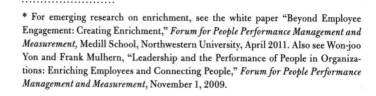

* For emerging research on enrichment, see the white paper "Beyond Employee Engagement: Creating Enrichment," *Forum for People Performance Management and Measurement,* Medill School, Northwestern University, April 2011. Also see Won-joo Yon and Frank Mulhern, "Leadership and the Performance of People in Organizations: Enriching Employees and Connecting People," *Forum for People Performance Management and Measurement*, November 1, 2009.

and more substantive as people, more capable of achievement—
precisely because they are.

To make enrichment palpable, the workplace experience
itself must provide team members with opportunities to grow
and express themselves as leaders. We encourage ground-level
decision making from day one by allowing team members a considerable amount of autonomy. In any shift, team members are
asked to open and close their section of the business on their
own using our operations cards, and they, not managers, determine for themselves when they've completed their tasks. "The
expectation is over there on the wall," we say, "so complete it
and let us know when you're going home." We also encourage
team members to resolve any unforeseen issues that come up
during the course of a shift. We give them a simple tool for decision making that we call "Issue—Purpose & Values—Solution":

As we tell new team members, there's no need to consult a
manager every time some unforeseen problem arises during a shift. To arrive at a solution, team members should run through the same analysis that I, the owner, would use, assessing the issue and potential solutions against the values we have defined for our-selves. As they'll discover, figuring out the right thing to do and understand-ing the relevance and nuance of our values can be quite a bit easier than it may seem at first.

SOLUTION

↑

**PURPOSE &
VALUES**

↑

ISSUE

Sometimes, just thinking about our values will suggest which solutions are valid and which aren't. In these cases, team members can take immediate action on their own. Megan, a Heart of House team member, injured her thumb and had difficulty working. She informed Stephanie, another team member, about the situation. Applying "Issue—Purpose & Values—Solution," Stephanie thought about our value to "support balance between home and work." Although this wasn't strictly speaking a home-work balance issue, the spirit of that value—giving people time that they need to feel fulfilled in their lives—was clear enough to Stephanie. Her solution: Volunteer to cover one of Megan's shifts so that her thumb could heal.

At other times, team members may find a situation ambiguous; a possible solution aligns with some values but not others. In such cases, they should choose the solution that serves the greatest number of values. Tim, a nineteen-year-old red-hat pro in our Heart of House, realized he wasn't scheduled to work during one of our big quarterly fund-raising benefits. He felt bad because he wasn't contributing, but he wasn't sure what to do. On the one hand, our home-work balance value might have suggested staying home and studying for his college courses. On the other hand, coming in to work for free even though he wasn't scheduled would serve our value of honoring "the relationships that connect our team, our guests and community." In addition, it would support our value calling for us to be "a profitable and fiscally responsible company." I'm proud to say that Tim did what so many others of our team members do and gave back to the community. In his analysis, he was able to come up with a strong solution that integrated multiple values.

Only when no clear solution exists should team members consult a manager, and even then, the manager will guide team members through a thought process rather than issue a judgment from on high. Kevin and Matt, Heart of House team members, had gotten into a pushing match at a previous job where they had worked together. Matt told Kevin, who was newer at Nick's, to wash dishes. Kevin thought he should be training on pizzas more, and he felt Matt wasn't living up to our value of treating team members with "dignity and respect" at all times. Scott, a manager, came in, assessed how the values applied in this situation, and supported Kevin. Aside from "dignity and respect," washing the dishes might have served our value of providing "a clean and safe environment for our guests and staff." In the end, Matt and Scott decided that providing a clean and safe environment did not require that Kevin wash the dishes at that exact moment. Putting their past differences aside, Kevin and Matt were able to serve another of our values: working "through support and cooperation" with other team members.

At all times, purpose and values serve as a guidepost, not a set of rules to which team members must abide. To quote a term made famous by George W. Bush, our team members are the "deciders"; it is they, not me or our managers, who ultimately bring our purpose and values and our culture to life. To deepen team members' understanding of our values, our team picks one of our values each day and focuses on it, connecting it with all the myriad tasks and situations that arise throughout the day. This extra attention prevents team members from ever perceiving that value as empty words. In their minds, they've lived that value by applying it to concrete circumstances.

Certainly you can't feel enriched in a job unless you believe your work is important. Because our "Issue—Purpose & Values—Solution" tool connects explicitly with the Nick's Experience, it gives team members a sense of leading on behalf of a greater calling. Team members understand that making a pizza, baking it, taking it out of the oven, slicing it up, and serving it to our guests isn't just a series of menial tasks; it's a way of enhancing peoples' lives. Something as simple as recognizing when a team member places their pizza in the oven correctly (for example, a double-decker goes in the back of the oven, and a gluten-free pizza goes in the front) supports our value of taking "pride in our commitment to provide quality service and a quality product," all in the service of giving our guests a community space where they can feel at home. I will personally recognize a team member for putting a gluten-free pizza in the front of the oven, identifying how important it is that we take pride in providing quality. In this and countless other instances, we explicitly define our daily operations in terms of our higher purpose and repeatedly affirm that definition throughout what is essentially a progressive and perpetual "onboarding" experience.

As inspiring as a sense of purpose is, team members must also believe that what they learn and experience on the job enhances their personal lives while leading over time to fulfilling, meaningful careers. With the aid of my expert coach Rudy Miick, we offer all team members early and progressive exposure to sophisticated leadership and communications frameworks that are seldom taught to entry-level employees. Training in communication skills begins at orientation and continues in a special leadership course called 301 that team members can sign up for after completing a single 200-level certification. Those wishing to be shift managers or Operating Partners can then apply to take our most extensive course, 401. Only 401, taught by our management team, requires another interview and selection on our part based on demonstrated leadership abilities. The other courses are open to everyone.

It would take too long to describe all the tools we teach, as well as the nuances involved in their application, so I'll highlight here a couple of the most important ones developed in orientation and in 301, and will save a discussion of the 400-level course for Chapter Five. One tool all new hires learn is what we call Be-Do-Have. The name plays on the idea that many people live their lives focusing first on *having*, then on *doing*, and finally on *being*. People who want to be leaders may think first about the nice car or big paycheck a leader enjoys. Then they think of things that a leader might have done to obtain the nice car, such as run a company or get elected to office. They believe that only when people have and do things associated with being a leader are they actually leaders; the "having" or the "doing" define the "being."

As we tell new hires, this mind-set can quickly lead to a victim's mentality and to excuses. "I'm not a leader," someone might say, "because so-and-so got promoted into the position I want." No, you *can* be a leader if you take control of your own destiny. Invert the hierarchy and start from the position of being. Decide what you want to be, and be that thing in your own mind. From there, make a point of behaving like a leader. Before you know it, the "have" part will fall into place.

Be-Do-Have is easy to understand, and for most of the young people we hire, it's a revelation. Another eye-opening tool we teach on the first day of orientation is Safe Space, a concept devised and owned by Rudy's company Miick and Associates. At all times, but especially when conflicts arise in the course of daily work, we hold Safe Space conversations that allow us to communicate more effectively and resolve issues without needless drama. Team members are taught to openly identify what we call the Moose in the Room, the sensitive issue (named for our logo, a moose head) that people are often afraid to discuss. They also learn to take ownership of their own opinions by speaking in the first person (for example, "I believe you're not cleaning up your area well enough" rather than "You're not cleaning up your area well enough"). Next we teach them to speak about observable facts and to avoid creating subjective meaning about facts ("You didn't clean up your station" instead of "You don't care about doing your work"); to pay attention to tone of voice and body language, not merely the words they're saying; and to check to make sure their communication is having the impact they intended, verifying it with the other party to the conversation.

Practicing and internalizing these skills leaves team members with new confidence. They feel capable of handling any issue that comes their way, both inside and outside Nick's. Yet Safe Space isn't merely a set of skills; it's a mindfulness practice that enables team members to become more aware of what and how they're communicating. Even after we teach these tools, we help team members practice them by encouraging them to use them on the job and coaching them through specific situations. One of our servers hadn't seen a fellow team member recently, so she said, "You never work anymore." Thanks to our coaching, she realized she was making her own meaning and not sticking to objective fact; maybe her teammate had been working at different times and our server just hadn't seen her. She immediately corrected herself and said, "I mean, I haven't worked with you for a couple of weeks." By practicing Safe Space and other tools, team members train themselves to remain more deeply aware, minute-to-minute, of what they're doing and thinking, channeling their speech and other behavior in ways that truly serve their interests.

Team members who are driven to further develop their leadership abilities progress to the 301 course, where they again encounter Be-Do-Have and Safe Space, only on a deeper level. We assign them a mentor (a trainer or manager) and issue them leadership "passports" for logging instances in which they've deployed our tools and values on the job. The mentor "signs off" on each story, validating the team member's retention of what we're teaching and giving the trainees a sense of ongoing accomplishment.

We also introduce several more-sophisticated organizational behavior tools that team members can practice on the job

Pages from a typical passport notebook.

and teach to others. Karpman's Drama Triangle, created by
psychiatrist Stephen B. Karpman,* helps team members understand the endless cycles of drama that flare up inside and outside the workplace—specifically, the three emotion-laden roles
people usually play: the perpetrator, who seems to have antago-
nized someone; the victim, who has seemingly been antago-
nized; and the rescuer, who has stepped in to fix the situation
and right wrongs. Team members discover that they can avoid
drama cycles if they first recognize the game for what it is and
identify the roles that they and others are playing. Keeping Safe
Space and "Issue—Purpose & Values—Solution" in mind, they
then consciously stop playing their roles. To resolve conflict-
laden situations as best they can, they keep their statements
focused on events in the present that they can influence (for
example, "Those two carry-out hosts, Jim and John, aren't stepping in when other team members need help with dishes"),
rather than on past events ("Jim and John *never* do anything. On
Christmas Eve, they were just standing around"). We also focus
on objective data we have in front of us ("Jim and John did not
ask the other team members if they needed help") rather than
any subjective meaning or interpretation we have about the data
("Jim and John didn't ask if others needed help because Jim and
John were angry"). We make direct, powerful statements, and
when all else fails, we walk away.

Another coaching tool we teach is one I learned from
Rudy. This framework alerts new hires to four roles people
play in coaching conversations: the ally, who asks questions;
the guide, who joins, side by side, the person being coached; the

---

* See karpmandramatriangle.com/index.html.

activist, who as the excited cheerleader applauds, inspires, and provokes; and the teacher, who conveys information by telling or lecturing. As we advise team members, each of these roles serves a helpful function in daily situations. The ally asks questions to keep the other person interested and involved; the guide acknowledges, answers, and builds; the activist keeps things moving and exciting for the person being coached; and the teacher conveys information as directly as possible.

For leaders and trainers, the important thing is to remain mindful, tracking what we're doing with the team or trainee; team members should use each component of this model to build energy and increase learning retention.

In general, we place a great deal of emphasis on cultivating mindfulness as leaders. We tell team members to stay constantly aware, both as individuals and as members of an organization, of how we are behaving and what signals we are sending. Team members learn that mindfulness drives learning—in a progression from unconscious incompetence to conscious incompetence (where we first become mindful of what we don't know how to do) to conscious competence (where we become mindful of what we can do) all the way up to unconscious competence. By becoming more mindful, we can effectively eliminate the phase of unconscious incompetence (where we don't even know what we don't know), facilitating learning and the path to A+ performance. Finally, we help team members become mindful of the connections between things, both organizationally (the relationship between individual, team, and company) and personally (the relationship between mind, body, heart, and soul). As leaders, we believe, all mindfulness starts by attending to ourselves holistically. To quote Richard Boyatzis in his book *Resonant*

Leadership: "When we attend to ourselves by developing our minds, taking care of our bodies, understanding and using the power of our emotions, and attending to our spirituality, however we choose to do so, we begin to reach our full potential as people."*

GROWING UP AT NICK'S

Individual team members who've been through our program confirm over and over again how much the communications tools described earlier improve their leadership abilities, both at home and in their personal lives. As black-hatted nineteen-year-old pizza cook Andy relates: "With 301 skills, I am able to communicate more with people. As a leader, I used to feel as if I was just bossing people around. Now with more of the 301 skills, I get people to do things without that feeling. I give more respect and *still* get things done." Rachel, a server who came to work with us in 2006, reports that she has found Safe Space useful in many situations. "I use 'I' statements all the time, even when my boyfriend and I are having a disagreement. I feel as if they do make a difference." And Georgie relates, "All the skills I learned through the training classes actually made me a better person, not just at work, but in my home life. You know, it made me a better parent in a lot of ways; it helped me get through tough times with my kids."

Individual tools might help, but do teammates come away from their overall work experience feeling enriched? The answer is yes, judging from the amazing personal growth and transformation many of our team members experience. Stephanie,

---

* Richard E. Boyatzis, *Resonant Leadership*, Boston: Harvard Business School Press, 2005.

one of our high-performance managers, came to work for us at sixteen. Shy and self-conscious, she kept silent during orientation, barely talking to others even during the team-building exercises. Beginning work at our carry-out counter, she found she was afraid to talk to guests. Yet she discovered that most guests really enjoyed talking with her and other members of the carry-out team. This helped build her confidence in dealing with other team members; she figured that if guests enjoyed speaking with her, other team members would, too. Soon her personality was blossoming at Nick's; she was having fun, learning, and doing a great job.

At eighteen, Stephanie signed up for 301. This time when she was thrown into a group of people she didn't know, she found it easier to participate without feeling nervous. She left 301 even more confident in her ability to solve problems and was able to readily step into difficult situations rather than ignoring them. Her growth continued, and a few years later, she underwent 400-level management training. Stephanie has been with us for six years and is now a genuine leader who feels at ease talking with everyone, team and guests alike. Even more exciting, she looks at her life as a constant opportunity to grow. "At this point, I can't wait to be pushed out of my comfort zone again to see what I can learn from it."

Matt, another longtime team member and the son of one of our servers, started at Nick's as a busser while just a high school freshman. He continued working throughout high school, enjoying himself so much that when several of his friends got jobs at Best Buy, he refused to join them, instead moving into our kitchen. "What I really loved was that I had to take charge of my own development, moving up and getting raises. There was a competitive atmosphere here; a lot of athletes worked at Nick's, and we all drove one another to do better. I got a lot of kitchen training, and I moved up pretty fast, learning new skills and positions. On paper the training system wasn't as defined as it is now, but the underlying theme and culture was always there—you drive it yourself!"

By his freshman year in college, Matt had become a senior cook and was training as a manager. He was leading thirty Heart of House team members on a shift, from high school kids all the way up to people in their fifties. "I felt confident, first and foremost, in the fact that I knew the business from the ground up. I'd learned every area of the restaurant, so that really helped. One of the first lessons Nick taught me in managing the Heart of House was being able to step out of it and look at the restaurant from 20,000 feet. 'Imagine you're sitting in a lifeguard's chair looking down on everything.' I still use that to this day. It really helps as you're running a busy Heart of House on a Friday or Saturday night. When the dough machine goes down, it's easy to get caught up in it, literally as well as figuratively!"

Matt continued to work at Nick's during college breaks. The summer before his senior year, he helped develop portions of our 201 training program for the Heart of House. After college, he got an internship with a life insurance company that turned into a job. Yet Nick's was in his blood, and he soon returned to intern as our bookkeeper. Receiving training from our CPA firm, he continued with us for five years before taking a job as assistant finance director for a resort property in California owned by Starwood. After only three months, his grateful boss promoted him, and he won an internal "leader of the quarter" award. From there, he took another leadership position at a smaller firm in the hospitality industry, Stonefire Grill in Los Angeles.

Reflecting on his career so far, Matt relates that he learned a number of vital lessons at Nick's. "First, I learned to take the lead in finding solutions to problems. I grew early on by realizing that it's important to take responsibility for doing something without being asked. This helps me today as a manager, for I'm still behaving proactively, modeling this behavior for those I'm managing, which leads them to respect me." Matt also emphasizes what he sees as a clear difference between our culture and others he's experienced when it comes to leadership. "Nick's had an expectation that everyone would be a great leader. That's not true everywhere. I've seen cultures where most people perform only to their job description and no more. They do the bare minimum. They don't engage in any creative thinking, don't ask, 'Is there another way I could do this? Is there a way I could help the other department work better?'" Today Matt is a thoughtful, inspirational leader, and he's on a path to success—in part because we gave him the freedom and support he needed to develop.

Not everyone on our team winds up becoming an award-winning leader, yet I can point to so many examples of young team members who have grown into amazing adults thanks to their leadership roles at Nick's. The most inspiring stories involve kids who rise up despite incredible odds. Justin, an eighteen-year-old, came to work for us when he was sixteen. I remember him as a skinny kid, energetic and ambitious, always willing to work hard, yet, like Stephanie, lacking the confidence to truly shine. After six months with us, he bloomed, first with our team and then with the guests. He didn't go to 301, but our managers remember that he responded really well to orientation, asking a lot of questions about how to use our communication tools and showing great eagerness to master them.

As of this writing, Justin has left Nick's to join the Marines and participate in basic training. Writing letters to the team from his base, Justin expresses his love of Nick's and reminds everyone to "stay focused on your purpose." What makes all this so exceptional is Justin's unique and sad backstory. The year before coming to work for us, Justin's mother had been sent to prison. Justin also sustained a serious injury that prevented him from playing football, which had been the main outlet for his anger. Whereas many kids under these circumstances descend into drugs or crime, Justin has used our tools to defuse conflict, make better decisions, and grow. He's developed into an all-star employee admired by peers, managers, and customers alike, not to mention me. "The coolest thing is how much of Nick's I've been able to apply in the Marines. Basic training for me was a breeze; I can't think of a single time when I was pushed to my limits. Everybody else was bored off their rockers in a class about military history, and because I was accustomed to being a part of a learning organization, I could always find something of interest to learn about. I'm focused, and I'm energized, and when I'm home on leave, I just can't stay away from Nick's."

LEADERSHIP AND THE HIGH-PERFORMANCE COMPANY

The mere fact that we can retain high-performance individuals like Justin, Stephanie, and Matt makes a huge impact on our bottom line. A manager who leaves early because he or she doesn't feel enriched can cost the company as much as a full year of salary. Based on my consultant Rudy's study of restaurant-industry norms, team members who leave can cost our company as much as $25,000 each, factoring in things like lost productivity and expenses associated with hiring and training new workers. I'm not sure I'll ever be able to calculate exactly how much we're saving because of our industry-leading turnover figures, but I know one thing: It's a lot!

Beyond retention, the leadership tools we teach raise the level of discourse throughout our company, allowing for much better teamwork, better customer service, and higher sales. As our server Rachel notes, "Teamwork is everywhere at Nick's. And I can tell you, the smallest amount of teamwork can make a difference; for example, any team member will rush out to help the servers by running food when it's busy. That directly impacts customer service. Guests appreciate it, and they come back. They also give bigger tips!" One of our team members recently described the teamwork she sees at Nick's as something beautiful, a work of art, especially in the Heart of House: "The great thing about being a pizza checker (the person assigned to check cooked pizzas for quality) on a very busy night is you get to look down the line and see everyone, all ten pizza makers, in sequence making a pizza. They're having fun while they work, and being a pizza checker is like being a conductor leading an orchestra, playing a beautiful piece, and that beautiful piece is a pizza, for our guests to enjoy."

Because such teamwork is the norm at Nick's, and our teams are accustomed to leading themselves, we can make do with far fewer high-priced managers. This saves us more than $80,000 per restaurant per year, based on an annual manager's salary of $40,000. In fact, we realized a total reduction in management wages of $104,274 (31.94%) between 2009 and 2010 alone due to shrinkage of our management team. Lauren, a server and bartender, notes that "empowerment and leadership training are the reasons for the team that we have. Our teams can run on their own because we don't need someone telling us what to do. In most companies, once the managers leave, things fall apart, because nobody knows what's next. Not here! We're all used to pushing ourselves to work faster and better, and to doing that together, as a team."

You might think making do with fewer managers means an uptick in theft, but in fact our careful screening process and leadership training *reduces* shrinkage. Theft is a clear violation of our purpose; our people are implicitly trained to not even *think* about swiping that extra bottle of gin behind the bar or a couple of bucks from the cash register. In addition, the sense of enrichment people feel yields a powerful feeling of investment in the company—and of being vested *in* the company. No one ever thinks about stealing from "The Man," because at Nick's, everyone's "the man" (something that our profit-sharing plan also reinforces). In fact, team members work on their own to *protect* what they feel is theirs, putting silent pressure on anyone they suspect of stealing. Since our teams work so closely together, new hires realize that their colleagues would feel deeply disappointed and betrayed if one of their own was to steal. In fifteen years of running Nick's, we haven't had to prosecute anyone for theft, and I'd have to think pretty hard to find a team member whom I had to fire for stealing.

Since managers don't have to police team members to make sure they're doing their jobs, they can spend more time interacting with guests. In the hospitality industry, sales come from anticipating guest needs, and the more time our managers spend checking on patrons to make sure they're enjoying their meals, the better the chance they'll return.

We also retain more of our managers for longer because they can enjoy themselves more at Nick's. As they'll tell you, interacting with guests is the "fun" part of their jobs—certainly more fun than the typical babysitting tasks, like walking next to a server confirming they're wiping the salt and pepper shakers.

When performance issues arise, we again save money by circumventing managers and having teams coach themselves. In 2010, we decided we wanted to improve the performance of our five- to six-person host teams. They weren't seating people as efficiently as we'd like, so tables sat empty for too long, while hungry guests suffered longer waits. We had a manager track their behaviors, but the manager didn't provide feedback or direction. Instead, we had our team conduct post-shift meetings, facilitated by the manager, in which each team member shared one thing they did well that had a positive impact on the team's performance, and one thing they would do differently if they could roll back the clock. As a group, they came up with a number of performance enhancements, such as seaters listening more carefully when the hosts announced where a particular party should be seated, so that the information didn't have to be repeated and guests could get their tables more quickly. The manager did offer his impressions, but only after the team members had talked it over, and only to support what they had said and go into greater detail about it. The process helped our team become more aware of their behaviors and their impacts, and it also helped the team members feel empowered to improve themselves.

Financial types out there might object, saying this way of empowering teams wastes money. If we're paying eight dollars an hour to our team members, and these post-shift meetings take fifteen minutes, and there are five hosts on a team, we're adding ten dollars per meeting to our labor costs to address a performance issue. Is that really fiscally sound?

I'd argue that it is. A high-priced manager can easily spend hours meeting with and disciplining individual staff members whom he or she thinks are falling short. This increases costs and prevents the manager from spending time on other work. Plus, the outcome of our post-shift meetings benefited us in many other, less direct ways. It improved our ability to get guests into seats faster, significantly enhancing our guest experience and sales. The meetings also got hosts to communicate among themselves more effectively, allowing them to root out other potential problems, such as a server who was falling behind on her tables. As a by-product of the meetings, hosts came up with new ways to have fun with guests on the microphones, entertaining them while they were waiting as long as an hour for a table. Finally, morale improved because rather than feeling ashamed for being disciplined or called out for doing something wrong, team members felt empowered to coach themselves to improve. Can we really put a dollar value on a positive work environment?

Training everyone as leaders also enables high performance by unleashing creativity and imagination. Recently, I was amazed to enter one of our restaurants and find a few servers brainstorming on their own about what we could do to make our late-night hours more profitable. During the winters, business slows after about nine at night, so these team members suggested bringing in acoustic guitar players or other kinds of entertainment to draw bigger crowds. Scott, one of our Operating Partners, joined the meeting, as did Joe, a nineteen-year-old manager and a musician. Hearing the ideas the servers had been bandying about, Joe helped clarify what kind of music and what instruments would align with our purpose. Alex, a server, then volunteered to come in and manage those nights during the week.

"So you mean you're volunteering to own those nights?" Scott asked.

"That's right," Alex said. "I'll do that because I think I can do a good job making sure this works for us."

Hearing that, I asked her, "How old are you again?"

"I'm twenty-two now," she said.

That just blew me away, given that she had just shown more leadership than many forty-year-olds do. I was also amazed to discover that our nineteen-year-old manager would possess such a mature understanding of our purpose and how to achieve it in a specific instance (a great example of applying our "Issue—Purpose & Values—Solution" model). All our Operating Partner was doing was taking notes! Keep in mind that most companies wouldn't let rank-and-file team members discuss issues like this; they'd hold a meeting with the marketing department and implement decisions from the top down. At Nick's, team members across the organization get a chance to innovate, making a difference for the company while building a sense of ownership and accomplishment among the team.

Specific innovations that emerge from the team sometimes have measurable financial impacts. When Kyle was only nineteen, he came up with an idea for a new product called beer nuggets. Kyle worked in our Heart of House, and he realized that we were throwing away a lot of scraps of dough. He suggested frying up these scraps, putting on some garlic salt and parmesan cheese, and serving them with olive oil or red sauce. "Sounds good," I said, "but you'll need to figure out portion size, pricing, and all that fun stuff." Kyle went away and did exactly that. Today we sell an eight-ounce portion of beer nuggets for $4.50. In 2010 we sold more than $21,000 of beer nuggets in our two restaurants, made with food we used to throw away. Here we have an innovation coming from a nineteen-year-old who dreamed up something that the forty-eight-year-old founder hadn't thought of, all because he was encouraged to think and behave like a leader.

Beyond innovations, we benefit simply because we have people willing to go the extra mile. On slow days our hosts volunteer to draw up signs and go out on the street corner, inviting motorists to "come on into Nick's." Servers and managers, upon hearing of a guest's house that has burned down, spontaneously pull together to bring them food. One team member got escorted out of a hospital while on a catering sales call (she was trying to sell our services to different hospital departments and didn't realize the hospital had a "no soliciting" policy) and in the process made several new contacts—including the security guard who took her to the door. Ultimately, training people to be leaders is tantamount to training them to operate well under Trust and Track. You're training them to be as proactive and aggressive as you are in driving the business—because they *want* to be.

A SCHOOL DISGUISED AS A COMPANY

As we've seen, building a high-performance culture in small businesses like mine means investing substantially in leadership training and then weaving that training seamlessly into the culture. Your company ceases to be merely a company and becomes a school disguised as a company. No one program or initiative is responsible for leadership training; rather, the whole culture is oriented toward training emerging leaders to succeed. One of our servers has likened Nick's to a teaching hospital, noting that here food rather than peoples' bodies becomes the occasion for and substance of the teaching. As another notes, the positive dynamic of learning and growing takes on a life of its own, becoming ever more deeply rooted in the culture and our people, even as we drive higher performance: "We take lots of time to learn, practice, coach, learn, practice, coach, and so on. Along the way, these giant lightbulbs go off for people, and they choose to do more next time, and to work more efficiently. Then they share that experience with someone else, providing that person with the same learning. We're using ourselves and our experiences as teaching instruments; we don't keep our learning to ourselves. Then, when there is enough self-confidence about owning their skills, people here choose to become trainers and perpetuate the learning at a much deeper level."

As we've seen, a company that becomes a school in disguise is a far more cooperative place than most companies today are. As an owner, I find that can take some getting used to. I will admit that on a bad day I find myself just wanting to be the boss and tell people what to do, only to find them pushing back with yet another new creative idea. *Jeez, do I have to listen to this?* I think. *I have things to do.* The thing is, I do have to listen to it. In a learning organization, team members at all levels develop a sense of ownership. They're putting themselves out there as leaders, pushing themselves and the company to be the best, so you have to be as excited as they are, and you have to meet or exceed the high-performance bar they're setting. It's no longer enough to be the guy with your name on the door and the keys to the place jangling in your pocket. You might legally still be the owner, and in my case, you might still have your name on the door, but you have to show respect to team members who feel that this place is an extension of them, too.

Structurally, a high-performance culture centered around

employee growth and development is a far flatter place. I'm proud of the fact, frankly, that we don't need nearly as many managers as most of our peers, and that they don't spend much of their time babysitting. The more completely I can empower my teams and develop everyone as leaders, the less oversight I need and the fewer managers I have to keep on the job. This is not to say that managers don't play an important role under a Trust and Track model. Instead of serving as police officers, managers enhance the growth process by serving as inspiring coaches and guides.

If you've ever tried to coach, you know it's not easy. Coaching requires just as much discipline as the skills and habits you're trying to instill. Organizations seeking to build high-performance cultures must thus take care to show managers how to coach well. The great lengths to which we go at Nick's to groom our managers as exceptional, inspiring coaches is the subject of the next chapter.

CHAPTER FIVE
Train Managers to Be Coaches

Just like people training in martial arts, yoga, meditation, or sports, team members in small businesses need guidance and encouragement if they are to flourish and build a high-performance culture. What they *don't* need are egotistical, authoritative managers standing over them and telling them what to do.

Like many small-business owners, I initially assumed I could hire good, experienced managers from outside, take time to show them the ropes, and then let them do their thing. But I found that most experienced managers—most *people*, in fact—were used to operating with rules, directives, hierarchies, policing powers, and the like. Even the nicest, most conscientious managers among the ones I hired fell into a pattern of control, making decisions by themselves, and thinking of others as subordinates. They were taking home the big salaries, and they didn't feel like they were earning their keep unless they acted like a conventional "boss." No amount of informal guidance or instruction from me seemed to help.

Today we submit managers to an intensive development program that teaches them the emotional intelligence and values required to coach others to thrive in our culture. We inculcate a collaborative coaching mind-set, helping managers understand that their greatest contribution comes not from a whiz-bang idea they might have, but from their ability to help *others* perform at their best. We encourage managers to serve as role models, practicing behaviors they expect of others rather than acting as if the rules don't apply to them. We also train managers to delegate rather than assume responsibility for everything. Above all, we discourage excessive ego because we don't want iconic leaders at any level of the organization. Rather, we want leaders dedicated to serving our entry-level team members.

A training program for managers seems like a tall order for a small business, but trust me, it pays off. We're blessed with a unique cadre of inspirational mentors who keep team members motivated, channel team members' energies toward self-improvement, and catch team members when they veer off purpose. I know our training works because I observe the close, emotional mentoring relationships that have blossomed between team members and managers. I've also seen individual team members excel in their work and personal lives; improved performance in our teams; a stronger, more pervasive culture; and, best of all, a reduced need for managers to drive our industry-leading business results. Our training system is so effective that our managers have gotten dangerously close to the ultimate goal in a high-performance culture: their own obsolescence.

LESSONS FROM MY FATHER

My dad is a big-hearted man who always showed the people who worked for him a great deal of compassion and generosity; yet as I've mentioned, he thought a manager's primary role was to serve as a police force—monitoring what were most likely untrustworthy employees who felt no sense of pride in the company. Dad didn't give team members a chance to grow as people, and he saw no point in coaching them on how to improve. He was willing to trust team members to work independently, but coaching, in his mind, was naive. It amounted to coddling people and getting "touchy-feely" when what they needed was toughness. People would take advantage of you if you nurtured them on the job; only a total wuss would think otherwise.

Whatever the merits of my father's hard-nosed approach, it did not lead to high performance in the workplace. Once when Dad was running his aluminum-siding business, he left me alone to install a drop ceiling in a client's large office. I was thirteen and could barely handle power tools. My father didn't spend time making sure I felt comfortable doing the job on my own; he gave me two minutes of instruction and left me to install the ceiling. When he returned eight hours later, he was disappointed to find I hadn't accomplished much. Not knowing the shortcuts, such as how to level from one side of the room to the other, I had been working in the most inefficient way. My father put all the blame on me: "What the hell? I was expecting you to finish this yourself, yet you barely did anything. What's the matter with you? Were you sleeping all day?"

I came away upset and disillusioned. I was trying my best, yet I had failed, and Dad hadn't even appreciated my effort. This scenario occurred repeatedly throughout my childhood, and not just with me. Dad would tell his team members what to do, trusting them to work on their own, yet he'd become frustrated when they didn't produce the desired results, all because he hadn't coached them. In the absence of positive feedback, people felt bad about their on-the-job experience, and they lost the motivation to improve. Rather than working up a sweat developing themselves, they bided their time and resented my father's authority. Under Dad's command-and-control regime, a lackluster workforce became a self-fulfilling prophecy.

For many years, I thought my father's approach was the only way leaders could interact with less-experienced colleagues. Only as I got into high school did I discover an alternate approach. As a football player and wrestler, I encountered great coaches who broke down tasks and behaviors step-by-step so my teammates and I could learn them faster and better and help the team excel. As our individual and group performance improved, I only became more motivated. I loved the discipline and the process of mastery, and I valued the support of the coaches who mentored me. My whole self-concept changed; for the first time, I felt confident and secure. Later, when I founded Nick's, I wanted people to work for me because they found it fulfilling and fun, not because they needed a paycheck. I wanted them to experience the joy that comes with excelling—the same joy a great football team feels when it wins a game, the feeling of truly believing in oneself. I sensed that my coaching approach to management would outperform my father's cynical command-and-control approach any day—in terms of both employee experience and bottom-line results.

My father's approach had another failing. Like others of his generation, he didn't see the need to articulate a purpose. He felt it was important to alert team members to job requirements, but he assumed that his position of authority meant he didn't have to explain *why* the business ran as it did. As I entered high school, I realized I didn't like remodeling houses with my dad or working in his pizza restaurant because I didn't know the point. Sports, by contrast, offered a sense of purpose. Participating was not merely about winning, but had a lot to do with team spirit, honor, and a desire to improve and do our best. When I started Nick's, I was determined that as a manager I would convey to team members the reason we were all here, even as I coached them on precisely what they needed to do to deliver on our purpose.

My concept of coaching deepened after meeting Rudy Miick and attending workshops at two retreat centers, the Gestalt Institute and Esalen. The Gestalt Institute's Cape Cod model really opened my eyes by setting forth an optimistic approach to coaching. That model teaches managers to be supportive, positive, and nurturing in every contact they have with the people they're coaching, affirming people when they get it right, inviting them to experiment and try new things, not getting down on people when they screw up. This was a revelation for me, since practically every sports coach I'd ever had, even the ones who took the time to explain why we needed to learn certain skills, had taken a tough-love approach. They had yelled, screamed, and sworn when I'd made a mistake, punished me with extra push-ups, tried to instill the fear of God in me.

Another dimension of the teachings of both the Gestalt Institute and Esalen that surprised me was their emphasis on mindfulness. I had always thought coaching involved focusing on the person you're coaching—how to strip away their weaknesses and build on their strengths. At Esalen, I exposed myself for the first time to yoga and other Eastern traditions that emphasized self-awareness and spiritual growth. Then I took the Gestalt Institute's weeklong workshop, which teaches that effective leadership proceeds from self-analysis and self-awareness. A good part of the workshop focused on working on ourselves as people, what the Institute calls "counter-transference" work. We explored how we made meaning of the world, how our own story—our past experiences, our family histories—colored each encounter we had. By cracking open a window onto ourselves, by learning how to observe ourselves in the moment, we could become better coaches. Once we comprehended our own behaviors, we could train ourselves to demonstrate for others how we'd like them to act—a simpler and much more effective way of offering guidance.

Visiting Gestalt and Esalen and seeing my own coach, Rudy, put his ideals into practice, I felt an inner drive to bring positive, mindful coaching back to my organization and my people. I began to apply the Cape Cod model in my daily work, integrating it in our meetings and teaching what I could to our managers. After a period of experimentation, I worked with Rudy and an Operating Partner to create and implement 401, a training system for managers. Together, using our "art" and "science" approach to training design, we defined what a Nick's manager does and then formulated the training from there.

We realized two things: First, the program couldn't just impart skills around coaching, since in order to coach well our managers needed to understand the art and science of all individual jobs at Nick's. Second, we realized that as far as coaching went, our 301 training program already captured the basic mindfulness and teaching skills our managers would need. We wound up organizing 401 as a compilation of 201 and 301, with some extra material relevant to managers (for example, how to handle cash, how to open and close the restaurant, additional readings and other materials about leadership) added in.

By 2005 we had put 401 in place and were requiring all managers to enroll, even those who had been with us for some time. I also went through the program, as did my Operating

Partner. We structured 401 as a formal course, with managers becoming "certified" in a series of specific job skills and positions, just as team members in our 201 program are. Like all team members, managers are assigned a mentor who is in charge of observing them, guiding them in their growth, and signing off on their progress. Because 401 incorporates both 201 and 301, it is oriented around experiential learning. Managers are given a thick binder to guide them, but in order to become certified, they don't simply mimic book knowledge; they perform the tasks we're teaching and are evaluated based on observation of their behavior. Although the course typically lasts ten weeks, the process is as flexible as our 201 program, and managers in training will certify at their own speed in areas like delegation, memorization of our purpose and values, how to run meetings, how to open and close the restaurant, and how to analyze the entire profit-and-loss statement. Most managers take ninety days to achieve all certifications and complete the course.

RESPECT THEM, AND THEY WILL RESPECT YOU

From day one, we redefine the managers' role by training managers to not make decisions and disseminate them from on high, but to empower team members to make more decisions for themselves and to grow in the process. As we run through the tasks managers typically handle, we show them how to open as much space as possible for team members to act, how to track team member behavior, how to celebrate when team members contribute to the Nick's Experience, and how to help team members realign when they veer off purpose. Applying their own wisdom and experience, and mastering communications tools like Safe Space, the Drama Triangle, and the Feedback Loop (described in Chapter Six), managers add value by reducing the time team members require to cycle between unconscious incompetence and unconscious competence. With the hands-on training we provide, every pre-shift meeting, every on-the-job conversation, every moment spent opening the restaurant office, and every shift change procedure becomes an opportunity to energize teams and inspire individuals to grow.

Redefining the manager's role also means imparting to new managers a vision of what excellence in coaching looks like. Any old coach can help low and average performers do better. What defines the outstanding coach is an ability to help people grow who already perform exceptionally well. When I think about great coaches, I think about football, especially Bill Parcells. The legendary New York Giants coach was able to corral the egos of players like Deion Sanders and help him up his game even further.

At Nick's we don't usually have to tame big egos, since we weed out those types during our hiring process. We do have to find ways to push all-star performers enough to keep them interested and engaged. Rather than feeling threatened by all-star talent, as some coaches are, our managers are taught to see such people as challenges. It's up to managers to push and become more creative in their coaching.

As I've suggested, the best way to achieve excellence is to model the desirable, on-purpose behavior you seek to impart. If you want pizza makers to place their pizzas in the oven more effectively, model that behavior yourself, identify or name what you are doing explicitly, and recognize the behavior in team members whenever you see it. Often when top performers become managers, they forget the middle step of naming their own outstanding behavior for others, since they have come to take what they do for granted. To excel as managers, we have to train ourselves to proclaim what we're doing—how we lean in when we talk to guests, how we smile and make direct eye contact, the smile in our voices as we answer the phone—as desirable behaviors for others to emulate; otherwise, they're lost as lessons.

Coaching through modeling might seem easy—just exhibit the desired behavior and let people around you drink it in. Look a little deeper, and coaching is the hardest thing you can do, certainly far harder than issuing directives. Modeling behavior well for others requires an incredible amount of self-awareness. At literally every moment, I need to comprehend my behavior enough to perform it well and articulate well to others what I'm doing. Every e-mail message I send, every conversation I have with others, every word I use becomes a potential learning opportunity for others. Am I walking up the stairs two at a time, conveying energy and enthusiasm, or am I plodding up slowly? What's my tone of voice? How about my body language? And am I aware of all this enough to point out to the seventeen-year-old newbie what I'm doing? We're asking managers not merely to show up but to serve as leaders of our organization, to be true believers of our message, and to exhibit that message in all that they do.

Our emphasis on modeling and coaching generally embodies a certain democratic ethic. Our business isn't perfectly or radically democratic; we have recognized sources of authority (me and our management team) as well as a certain number of directives and guidelines from on high that define excellence, structure what we do, and channel energies toward high performance. We do tend toward cooperation, though, to the extent that we don't have one standard of behavior for managers and another for team members. To coach well, managers must hew even more closely than everybody else to common standards we're trying to set. As we tell managers, every behavior we perform has to communicate to the team that they are accepted and supported, and that we want them to be successful. It's worth noting what's not on the list: that the manager is a figure to be worshipped, the sole source of authority in all situations, someone who should never be questioned.

We do offer strong feedback, but we take care to avoid yelling, name calling, and other ugly behavior deriving from a sense of superiority. Also, if conflict arises between a team member and a coach, or between a team member and me, we don't automatically ascribe fault to the team member. On the contrary, we start by asking what the coach or owner could be doing better. As we say in 401: "There are no team-member issues; there are only leadership issues."

In the film *Peaceful Warrior*, Nick Nolte's character says, "This is a service station. There is no higher purpose than service." That's precisely the ethic we seek to instill among our managers. The whole 401 program is set up to cultivate modesty, selflessness, and a lack of ego, because we think that translates into good coaching. For managers who come to us from outside, 401 can be a humbling experience. As they go through the 201 training, every manager starts on the line making our product. At the end of every shift the highly paid manager, just like every other team member, has a conversation during which his trainer provides feedback on what he did well and what he needs to do better. The new manager's certification isn't up to another manager or me; it's entirely up to a trainer, who could be an eighteen-year-old kid.

As one of our new managers recently told me, "In all my

years working at Panera Bread and Lonestar Steakhouse, I was never trained and held accountable by team members this young. It was very humbling, and quite the eye-opener [when it happened to me here]. They wouldn't cut me any slack just because I was going to be an Operating Partner. That was just as impressive to me, because it indicated just how strong the culture was at Nick's."

Upholding our desire to retain elements of democracy, or at least a more cooperative form of hierarchy, our managers learn to approach conflict openly and to accept that their perspectives might not hold sway as absolute truth. They also learn to reflect openly on their own behavior in public settings with team members. Lots of companies hold check-in sessions before and after shifts, but at Nick's we train managers to put aside any pretense to perfection and state exactly which of their own behaviors they would like to improve. Following our teachings in 401, and modeling behavior for team members, a manager might say, "What I did well tonight was step into a dialogue with guests who were really upset about having to wait for their table longer than we first said. What I want to enhance about my performance is to set the shift up better in the first place, paying attention to any signs that we didn't have the right people in the right places. Tonight we had too many people training at the host desk without enough trainer support on a $12,000 shift."

Being a strong coach ultimately flows from being a strong, mindful person. We expose managers to readings and inspirational quotations that raise their awareness of themselves and of their connections with the wider world, stressing especially the importance of constant and ever-deepening mindfulness. As Richard Boyatzis notes in his book *Resonant Leadership*, "Great leaders are emotionally intelligent and they are mindful: They seek to live in full consciousness of self, others, nature, and society." I also use Karl Weick and Kathleen Sutcliffe's book *Managing the Unexpected* as a teaching tool for my Operating Partners. As Weick and Sutcliffe write, "Mindfulness must be treated as a culture as well as a set of principles that guide practice."* As I've suggested elsewhere, what we're ultimately doing is creating a culture of mindfulness, and in our 401 training, we deploy our manager-coaches as both agents and exemplars of that enlightened perspective.

Finally, one notable feature of our 401 training is its usefulness as a screening mechanism for new hires. Just as the 201 course does, 401 helps us weed out those relatively few managerial hires who don't fit our culture well yet who managed to make it through our hiring process.

One new manager, Jim, interviewed well and said the right things. I think he really cared about people and somewhere deep inside he did want to coach, but he was never able to get past his own ego. Once during his 401 training period, he became frustrated at a team member and erupted into a fit of yelling. I took Jim aside and asked what was going on.

"They're not respecting me," he said.

"What do you mean?"

"Well, I'm a boss. They need to respect me."

"They don't need to respect you," I told him. "You need to respect them. If you do that, they *will* respect you."

Jim shook his head. "Is that really true? If I focus on respecting them, then they're going to think they're the boss."

"Well, yeah, they are the boss," I said. "You're here to guide and coach them. That's the whole point."

---

* Karl Weick and Kathleen Sutcliffe, *Managing the Unexpected* (San Francisco: Jossey-Bass, 2007).

As we came away from this conversation, I realized Jim just didn't get the concept of Trust and Track on a deep level. He got it in theory, in his head, but if he had really internalized the essence of our culture and the way we envision manager-team member relationships, I wouldn't have had to spend so much time explaining it to him.

As Jim's 401 training continued, others kept telling me he wasn't incorporating our training well. Jim had days when he seemed to take my coaching to heart, but on other days, during high-powered shifts, emotion dominated his behavior and his discipline failed. He found it frustrating to coach his teammates; on one occasion he said that it was "too much work for me to slow down when we've got guests waiting out the door and think about what I'm going to say." I also noticed he was having a hard time adopting our mindfulness practices; when we meditated at manager meetings, as we always do, he excused himself, claiming that his mind "is going too fast" and that he "can't sit still quietly like that for that long of a time." He seemed to be losing motivation in our training process. By the time Jim completed 401, it was clear to everyone—including Jim—that it was time for him to go. I asked him if he felt that Nick's was the place for him. He said no and resigned from the company.

EXPERT COACHING AND HIGH PERFORMANCE

When I try to calculate the benefits to our culture of teaching managers to be coaches, I think first of extraordinary coaches in sports who ultimately are judged by their teams' performance and the characters of the individuals they develop on their teams. I've already relayed our organizational results, and I have to think they reflect at least in part the ability of our coaches to inspire individual team members. As for the character of our team members, you've already met several of them and heard their stories. Trust me, there are many more where those came from.

Even managers who fail with us leave our organization as better coaches than when they walked through our doors. Managers who stay for even just a year or two become extraordinary coaches by most standards, inspiring team members to achieve great things and serving as transformational figures. As a twenty-year-old busser told me, his first trainer, our manager Alex, dazzled him by his ability to lead by example. "He would do a great job explaining how to do a certain task and then execute it just how he explained it. The reason he had such an impact on me was because he was my first trainer and always modeled our purpose and values in his work. He set expectations for me not only in bussing, but in my career at Nick's. The other thing that made him an exceptional leader is that he wanted to see me be the best I could be and help me achieve it. As soon as I started working with Alex I thought to myself, 'I want to work just like he does.'" Our managers invigorate their sixteen- and seventeen-year-old teammates, serving as the role models these kids crave and making them understand that our organization cares about them and their growth.

Managers also tell me that their training and ongoing experience at Nick's has allowed them to become more aware of their own minds and actions. Amy, who has been with us for more than six years, describes how she initially reacted defensively when her managers coached her by lecturing her on what to do (a response common to Gen Y workers). During a Safe Space conversation, she relayed her defensiveness to her coach, who surprised her by telling her that he felt safe offering her direction because of their strong relationship. Even after this conversation, Amy still had trouble receiving her coach's guidance, but she was working on it. "My ability to hear feedback has shifted in that while I am also working on my own stuff, I am now able to hear direct, teacher-style feedback in an entirely different way—the way my coach intends it." I'm impressed that Amy has improved, and even more impressed that she is able to be so clear and introspective about her patterns.

I have seen my own coaching abilities improve. When I worked in construction, I was always the high performer who wanted to outwork everyone else. I transferred that mentality to the restaurant, pushing myself and pressuring others too hard. "It's so tough working for you, Uncle Nick," my niece Gina and nephew Dominic would say. As I studied our coaching models, I learned how important it was to build a relationship and establish common ground with the team. By developing people rather than just ordering them around, I wound up authorizing them to make decisions on their own, without me even needing to be there. It's been an amazing growth experience for me, and because of 401 I'm able to share it with our managers and disseminate it throughout our culture.

We see so much more delegation going on between managers and teammates and, as a result, more energized and efficient operations. One of our managers, Scott, applied our training by developing a teammate, James, to help him lead a team in our Heart of House. Scott then asked James to develop his own cadre of leaders to run the Heart of House. Now we have a whole army of well-trained, entry-level team members running our busy shifts, which allows Scott and some of the managers-in-training to spend more time talking to guests and building sales. "Working a shift is more fun," Scott relates, "and we get better results. When I was at my old job, I led a high-performing team, but as a leader I had to make things up as I went. Here the leadership tools I need to move the team forward were already developed. At my old job, if I wasn't present, the team moved slower and wasn't as hungry to develop as individuals. Here, our entire culture supports team leadership and self-development on the part of team members, so performance increases faster, without me having to stand over people."

Our 401 training also contributes by training managers to avoid needless drama. Amy, one of our managers, had a conversation with two team members, Sammi and Lindsay, both around twenty years old. The young ladies approached Amy at the start of a shift and said, "We want to be like you and not go into drama." Applying skills she learned in 401, Amy corrected them and said, "Are you kidding? I'm in drama all the time. What I'm doing is remaining mindful and catching my response so I don't *act* out of drama. When you start to react emotionally, your heart races, your cheeks get flushed—it shows up in your body. Over time, you train yourself to stop and then wait through whatever your cycle time is before acting. That's how you don't act out of drama."

Later during the shift, the two young ladies happened to be present as Amy grew frustrated with one of the bussers. "I started to say something," Amy remembered, "and then I stopped. I said, 'No, I'll check in with them later.'"

Seeing this, Lindsay said, "You just caught yourself in drama."

"You're right," Amy responded, "I did. Instead of venting, I just went right out of it."

Sammi and Lindsay didn't suddenly learn right then and there how to stop reacting emotionally on the job or in their lives, but the seed had been planted, and in an especially power-ful way—through example. "Over time, in the ensuing shifts, I saw behavior change," Amy said. "They started to get it. And as a result, things moved more smoothly around here. It really helps that we as managers walk the walk in our coaching. That's so critical."

Overt conflict between managers and team members is extremely rare at Nick's, which contributes mightily (if unquan-tifiably) to high performance. Issues do arise, but they're handled better and more efficiently. Once, a conflict broke out between Imelda, one of our best and longest-working servers, and my daughter, Michelle. Imelda is the breadwinner in her family, so money is important to her. Our hosts are trained not to leave money on the table; they're supposed to pick it up and take it to the server. Michelle was working as a host, and she had picked up a check on the table and looked through the money, trying to figure out who the server was by checking the name on the receipt. Imelda saw Michelle holding the money in her hand and thought she had taken some of the tip. Even though Michelle was my daughter, Imelda took a risk and confronted her about it. She accused Michelle instead of asking her to explain her behav-ior, thus violating two key tenets—checking our own "meaning making" and making an "I" statement. In my capacity as coach, I sat down with Imelda, taking her through Safe Space. Imelda was totally unaware that she was already accusing Michelle and that she had never even asked Michelle what her intention was. This problem, which might have festered and led to resent-ments, was quickly resolved.

The mere fact so many team members ask for coaching, as Samantha and Lindsay did, testifies to the effectiveness of 401. Applying their new skills, coaches are making themselves accessible to team members and giving people permission to approach them. Team members view them not as hard-nosed authority figures like my father was during my childhood, but as resources to consult. It's also worth noting that most team members request coaching around people skills and the mastering of emotions rather than around simple, job-related tasks. Because we have well-trained coaches, because we've oriented our whole workplace around personal development, and because we've broken down and trained basic job skills so well, we're able to operate at a higher level of learning. Our people aren't working on putting enough cheese on the pizza or setting the table properly; they've mastered that stuff, and now they're comfortable turning to our managers to work on the "softer," people-related skills that allow them to deliver the Nick's Experience with every interaction.

The deep, authentic relationships that form between coaches and team members also reveal the efficacy of training. Alan, a young team member, told me of a time when he was having trouble certifying in a position. Other team members were bragging that they had learned the skills in eight shifts, whereas it had taken Alan fifteen or sixteen. "One of the managers, Jake— he noticed how much it was bothering me because some of the guys were sort of bragging. He pulled me aside and he goes, 'You know, it might have been taking you long, but you're doing a really great job. Everything else you're doing is good and you're doing a great job. Keep it up!' And at that time, it made me feel really good about just being here. I'll never forget it, and from then on I really looked up to Jake." The sheer number of connections like this one that I've observed helps explain our low turnover. Our team members don't want to let our coaches down, since the coaches command their respect.

"DON'T YOU HAVE A BOSS HERE?"

For hard-nosed realists, linking a specific program like 401 with a culture of high performance might still not be enough to make a business case for implementing the program. But consider this: We save enough on managers' salaries every year to more than cover our outlay. We spend about a two-week salary per manager to run 401 if that manager rose through the ranks with us, and about one month's salary per manager if that manager came from outside. That's not nothing, but it's not a huge outlay given the program's impact on our culture. Today some of our shifts don't even have a manager on duty. Sometimes, in fact, we just have a manager on duty so the guests can feel they're talking to someone important. Guests are often stunned to discover how well our restaurants operate without managers. Recently, one of our servers was closing the restaurant, and a guest at one of her tables wanted to talk to a manager. She replied, "I am the manager."

"What do you mean?" the guest asked. "Don't you have a boss here?"

Flattening the structure always remains the objective under Trust and Track; whenever you have managers at all, even with a good training program, you run the risk they'll try to create value by telling people what to do. Some days I dream about a totally democratic workplace comprised entirely of teams and trainers without bosses. I don't know if most businesses will ever be able to make do without conventional managers, but I do know that in the twenty-first-century economy, success even in small, local businesses originates largely in the performance of creative teams. Individuals work better when they are motivated intrinsically, and so leaders who can get individuals excited about their work and help them see the meaning in it become more and more important. It makes no sense to hire managers to serve as babysitters. Train managers to bring out the best in others, to inspire them to surpass what they think they can accomplish as people, and you get high-performance results.

CHAPTER SIX
Inspire Good Behavior

We've talked about how we get the coaches we need for a high-performance culture, but what exactly do they do on the job? Here's a hint: behavior, behavior, behavior! It's a basic fact of human nature that even our subtlest actions—how we greet people, our gait, how we sign e-mails—send messages about who we are. When building a company culture, such messages are pivotal because not only does each team member's behavior affect what his colleagues and supervisors think about him; it affects what customers, investors, and others outside a company think of the entire organization. Anyone striving to build a high-performance culture must motivate team members to think carefully about even the smallest behaviors so that every action expresses purpose and values and supports the culture.

At Nick's, our established practices, tools, and guidelines allow coaches to monitor or track team members' behavior on the job in a structured way, so that they can then intervene to shape behavior. I'm not talking about setting up intrusive security cameras everywhere, but rather organizing our coaching around the close observation, person to person, of what our team members actually do while they're working. We deploy observation in a positive way, encouraging on-purpose behavior that strengthens our culture. By rewarding people for good behavior, rather than reprimanding them for bad, we instill a sense of pride and accomplishment in them that in turn inspires them to do well all the time, even when we're not looking.

As a parent, I can attest to the power of positive reinforcement, and I see it as a manager as well—especially when it comes to our younger team members. When we tell teenagers what they're doing well, their self-esteem skyrockets, and you can actually *see* their confidence in the way they walk and talk, in their posture and tone of voice. It's no exaggeration to say that people at Nick's welcome the attention managers and trainers pay to the nuances of their behavior, because they know that we're helping them improve and be more of who they already are. "Giving feedback and tracking other people is a normal thing to do around here," our pizza maker Shanda says. "Our managers are great, and in fact that's one of the things I love about this place; we're all free to help others do better."

As easy as it may sound, behavior is hard for our managers to track. Behaviors on the job are so numerous and interrelated that they can seem overwhelming to ponder. In just a few minutes, a pizza puller (a person working our pizza ovens) might spin several pizzas in one of our six ovens, scan the several dozen pizzas currently cooking, check for tickets with multiple pizzas to assure they come out in order, and coordinate with servers, the team members who cut the pizzas, and our carry-out hosts— all while greeting guests as they walk into our open kitchen. Considering the demands placed on just one team member, you can understand why typical quantitative observation tools— marketing and human resources metrics like customer satisfaction, attrition, and job satisfaction—provide only the broadest measure of what's going on and don't even begin to capture the richness and nuance of actual, on-the-job behavior.

At Nick's, we don't pretend to track every last thing our team members do (with almost 200 people on staff, how could we?), nor do we rely strictly or even primarily on formal quantitative measures. Instead, we provide our managers with powerful frameworks for assessing qualitatively what our people are doing and how precisely they're doing it.

Very often we think we can't change behaviors. "People will be people," managers say. "They either have it or they don't." Yet so much of our behavior as both individuals and organizations seems ingrained only because we're unaware of it. When we do become aware, we often *can* change.

I've seen so many cases at Nick's of young adults who've come in tentative and withdrawn and who, thanks to close monitoring of their behavior, have blossomed into superstar team members any company would welcome. Our strong financial performance, off-the-charts customer loyalty, and other external measurements testify to the power of a culture built around collecting data about behavior and then celebrating success. Creating the culture we want is possible, but it requires that everyone be aware of and responsible for their own actions.

NO MORE TRUST AND HOPE

In 2003, when I underwent my personal transformation, and when we first began to take our culture to the next level by implementing purpose and values, I didn't appreciate the need to track. I had dismissed the notion of any kind of accountability around behavior and was determined to eradicate behaviors and ideas I associated with my dad's cynical view of workers.

Tracking performance seemed synonymous with being "mean." It would be far better and nicer, I thought, for managers to act as sympathetic therapists, asking questions of people, listening to them, showering them with compliments, and waiting for them to change and develop on their own time. It's embarrassing to remember, but week after week, I sat and listened to team members' problems, trying to help them understand how their perspective reflected their childhood experiences, but not spending any time observing and evaluating their performance.

One server, Beth, had five kids and was going through a divorce. She'd cry at work, and in my desire to be a nice boss, I covered her tables and then we talked over her problems. A bartender, Debby, had gone through a divorce, had two girls, and was struggling to balance her job at Nick's with another one. As a compassionate boss, I allowed her to show up late for work and miss shifts without any consequence, again seeing it as my role to talk her through her rough times.

My approach had become based on trust and hope rather than on Trust and Track. Predictably, it didn't work too well. I was working harder and doing other peoples' jobs, yet performance was flagging. Team members weren't finishing projects on time; they were arriving late for their shifts; they were forgetting to perform necessary tasks when opening or closing the restaurants. When my managers failed to account for all our food and beverage costs period after period, I blamed it on our inventory system and made excuses for people. Not once did I admit to myself that it was the people who were screwing up. Bottles of booze went missing, but I never once pointed the finger. I was knowingly allowing the business to lose money, all because I refused to demand performance.

All this ended in 2006 and 2007, when I experienced a

breakthrough as a leader. I learned in a yoga retreat about the cosmic egg, the Himalayan concept that predated yin and yang. According to this concept, the line between the opposites of love and fear (or any two opposites) is karma—the action one takes. If that action doesn't draw on both love and fear in equal measure, poor results will follow. At about the time I was pondering the notion of balanced action, I went to a speech by the Dalai Lama in which he talked about tough love, the idea that sometimes a little spank on the butt is good. *Wow*, I thought, *that's the answer!* I needed to project leadership that came out of both love *and* fear. Fear yields management actions around command and control; love yields management actions around trust and hope. I needed something in the middle; I needed to trust and track.

I realized we weren't in business to assure the personal development of our team members, nor was it my responsibility to serve as a therapist and solve everyone's deep issues. We were in business to make money. Sure, we could provide opportunities for personal development, but if people weren't choosing to develop themselves, if they were choosing to behave in a manner that hurt the company, then they were choosing to not be part of the company.

I may have been telling Beth that she needed to have more discipline with her kids, her ex-husband, and her life, but by making excuses for her or looking the other way whenever she failed to meet my expectations, I was unconsciously encouraging her to do the opposite. I might have helped Beth feel a little better about herself, but she was still stuck at her same level of development and self-awareness. Her relationship with her family didn't get much better, and she certainly wasn't improving at work. She wasn't realizing the deeper sense of confidence and satisfaction that comes with really working to better oneself, overcome obstacles, and attain goals. Unfortunately, Beth's stalled growth mirrored the experience of other team members and of our company as a whole. We needed to shift gears—and fast.

USING COMMUNICATION TOOLS TO TRACK AND CELEBRATE

Today we still trust people, but we've also developed processes for tracking actual behavior, so that we can hold people accountable for their own progress. Surprisingly enough, the main observational tools are the very same communication tools described in previous chapters. Deployed by our managers, Safe Space and Karpman's Drama Triangle function as sophisticated tracking tools in disguise, allowing our managers to become, in effect, amateur anthropologists, keen observers of human behavior. In orientation, a new team member will learn how to use Safe Space as a communication tool to work through conflict. In our leadership training, by contrast, we have managers and trainers go deeper and learn how to use Safe Space to track behaviors. In day-to-day encounters with team members, our managers and trainers ask: What is a person's body language and tone of voice? Is he or she using "I" statements? Is he or she being sarcastic? Is he or she making meaning or tracking data? We specifically hold our trainers responsible for acting as "moose slayers"; they track minute behaviors to determine what the "Moose in the Room" is (see Chapter Four), so that they can then seek out the Moose and dispense with it. When our managers interview prospective hires, they deploy Safe Space to understand the smallest elements of their behavior and determine if they're aligned well with our purpose and values.

Karpman's Drama Triangle functions in much the same way

as Safe Space—as a means to structure personal observation. Managers use the Drama Triangle to remain present and stay out of drama, recognizing that letting ourselves get drawn into "playing the game" causes us to be inauthentic, disengaged, and unfulfilled. But deploying Karpman's Drama Triangle also allows managers to track and analyze peoples' behavior along the three positions that make up the triangle. Are people around them and are they themselves behaving or speaking as victims caught up in the past? Are they behaving or speaking as controllers or perpetrators who are instigating an issue? Or are they behaving or speaking as rescuers, people who are trying to "save" the world and, in particular, the victim? By its very nature, the Drama Triangle serves managers as an analytic way to track behavior—and ultimately, to help shape it in desirable ways that serve our culture.

For tracking to really work, you need to go beyond the superficial behaviors and the things people say and monitor the underlying subtleties and psychology. At Nick's, we advise managers on the "art" and "science" of tracking intuitively the energy levels a person exudes. On the art side, we tell managers to determine whether a new host is speaking to guests in tight, clipped sentences (suggesting nervousness, perhaps) or if they're speaking in a vibrant, flowing manner that lets their energy out. On the science side, we train managers to ask: Are servers smiling or making eye contact out of excitement or happiness? Are they phrasing things in the manner of a question due to a sense of uncertainty? Are three teenage servers in a pre-shift huddle holding a side conversation while the main conversation is going on? Once aware of energy states, managers can act to mold behavior. Tim, a manager-in-training, noted that it was too quiet in the Heart of House, and he sensed that people were becoming bored. When Kip, a dishwasher, brought back dishes from the dining room, Tim started chanting, "Kip! Kip! Kip!" That did the trick; soon everyone was laughing and having fun again.

What we call Moments of Magic also serve as a tool for managers and trainers to structure their observations. Moments of Magic include several behaviors that our team members train themselves to perform: greeting everyone you see within five steps of you; greeting everyone you see entering and exiting the restaurant; answering the phone within three rings; and subjecting all behavior to the Grandma Test (that is, would your grandma approve of what you're doing?). Our managers and trainers can use the Moment of Magic framework as a starting point for assessing the behavior of team members. Are they always greeting people around them? Are they applying the Grandma Test to each and every behavior?

A similar system could easily translate to any white-collar office. As our company has grown and we've employed more executives, I've started tracking very small behaviors around the office, such as how people handle e-mails. Once I noticed that Jill, a member of our accounting department, seemed to craft e-mails in a way that suggested disengagement. She started her e-mails requesting information or action from people without acknowledging whom she was addressing (that is, without writing an opener such as "Dear Bob"), and she never clearly specified what she was talking about. I perceived that she was being too "nice"; not wanting to alienate new colleagues, she seemed afraid to hold specific people accountable to her. I let her know she should name the people from whom specifically she needed commitments and state exactly what commitment she sought, because otherwise people wouldn't take action. As soon as she made this subtle switch in her e-mail behavior, I celebrated by telling her how much I appreciated it. Over time, her e-mails became more specific and useful. I continue to track how energetic people are in e-mails (punctuation such as exclamation points suggest enthusiasm, whereas filler words tend to suggest lackluster attitude), how long it takes people to respond, the specificity of what people say, and the willingness of people to make and meet commitments. Are people paying attention to how they sign their e-mails? Do they do it with purpose? We want our white-collar folks to be just as exuberant, present-minded, and outgoing as our servers in the restaurants, even though they may not interact directly with guests.

When tracking behavior, it's important to remind team members why a specific action is desirable by tying it back to a larger purpose or value. Remember the "naming" our managers perform in the process of modeling good behavior? Another big part of a manager's job is to acknowledge good behavior at the exact moment they see team members performing it. "Great job with the smile within five steps." "Nice work getting the right amount of cheese on those pizzas." If a team member says to another, "I'm coming up behind you" or "thank you," we'll connect the behavior to a specific company value by saying, "Nice work treating the other team member with dignity and respect." That way, team members understand they belong to an explicit culture rather than one in which behavior is left primarily to chance. Our leadership passport tool, described in Chapter Four, allows emerging managers and trainers to practice connecting their own actions with our values. After weeks spent filling out their booklets, they're well prepared to view the actions of other team members through the prism of our values.

When our employees behave well, their effort usually manifests in quantifiable data, including tips, sales, and customer requests for a particular server. To replicate this behavior in others, we use such data as an indicator and then work backward to figure out what behavior led to that result. Recently, Jen, one of our servers, was selling add-on food items like crazy. When a manager inquired how she had been so successful, Jen explained she had been telling guests how delicious our Italian beef sandwich was when prepared on garlic bread with cheese, and that her enthusiasm made people want to buy more of it. In another instance, a carry-out host who answers our phones was asked how she increased her check average. The answer (which we've since integrated into our training) turned out to be as subtle as offering mozzarella sticks to guests in an open-ended way: "What munchies can I get for you tonight—mozzarella sticks or our delicious bruschetta?" In both cases, managers applauded positive behavior and encouraged team members to share their enhancements with others so the whole team could improve.

Meetings provide an excellent venue for publicly validating behavior and disseminating these emerging "best practices." After Jen had so much success with add-on food items, we asked her to share with everyone in a pre-shift huddle the personal statement she was delivering to guests about how to eat our beef sandwich. Likewise, in our executive meetings, I look for opportunities to recognize behavior I want to see more of in my Operating Partners. When one of my Operating Partners, Scott, was failing to track other peoples' action steps and deadlines in our meetings, I looked for opportunities to encourage the right behavior. When at one meeting, he asked one of the other managers, "When are you going to have that done?" I recognized Scott for asking that question, and predictably, he has gotten much better at holding people accountable for getting things done on time.

In addition to moment-to-moment tracking, we also use various forms of structured feedback to validate good behavior. Our Feedback Loop is a two-way conversation managers have with teammates, typically at the end of each training shift. This is sometimes a substantial, ten-minute conversation in which we analyze, in depth, a positive behavior together. Performance Feedback is a one-sided assessment of behavior, perhaps ten to twenty seconds in length, given at any time by a manager, right at the moment a behavior occurs. Direct Feedback is similar to Performance Feedback in that it's given in the moment, but it's typically just one quick phrase or sentence presented to the team member about his or her behavior (for example, "Great smile"; "Nice carry of those beers"; "Perfect pizza you've made").

As one part of our Feedback Loop, which takes place both in writing and conversationally, we ask team members to name one thing they think they did well; we'll agree with what they say and build on it. The manager or trainer then names another behavior that he or she thought the team member did well. As a result of this conversation with a manager, the team member comes away feeling validated and more conscious of something that quite often they didn't even know they were doing well. The Feedback Loop also trains team members to observe their behavior on their own, which may not come naturally at first. Sometimes I'll encounter a server or hostess at the end of a shift and ask them to name one thing they've done well. Guess what? They can't do it! They unconsciously go right to the things they did wrong. But by having managers celebrate their good behaviors each night, they grow more and more aware of how they're acting in the moment.

In other restaurant companies, General Managers rarely venture out on the floor; they sequester themselves in their

Host – Seater Training – Certification Feedback Loop

Trainer: Please complete the following information after each training shift.

Trainer Name: **Kelly / Amy**   Trainee Name: **Caroline**

Date: **5/5**   Shift Sales: **3800**   Shift Follow # **10**

Certification Shift (Circle one) **YES** NO   Online Quiz Score: _____
(If YES see Certification Process Wrap Up) 1st   Retake on: _____ Score: _____

This form is a tool for you, the trainee, to support your development. All feedback recorded here must be very specific and directed toward only your performance in your shift.

TRAINEE	TRAINER
What's one specific thing I did well tonight?	One specific thing you did well tonight was:
I made great guest connections + stayed busy.	Great improvement on guest approach.
What's one specific thing I can do differently in my next shift to enhance my performance?	One specific thing you can do differently in your next shift to enhance my performance is:
Still work on paying attention to hearing table #s the first time they are said.	Making eye contact + listening to where the party's going

Trainee's Comments:
Slow shift, but I really supported my teammates with pre-busing + checking lobby.

Trainer's Comments:
Great job staying busy on a slow shift!

On Your Next Shift:
Listening to where party's going   Manager's Signature *AW*

A typical certification feedback form, this one for a host who seats our guests.

offices and monitor operations abstractly through the numbers. If they want to change the way things are done, they do so by issuing broad directives to everyone, without taking behavior into account. When our Operating Partners are on duty during a shift, they're roaming our restaurants, scrutinizing what our team is doing and giving positive feedback. We have managers perform what we call a Figure Eight through the building, making a lap around the restaurant, touching tables and talking to guests, and then taking a second lap to focus on the team. Hour after hour, our managers get into the nitty-gritty behavior that comprises our culture, which allows them to influence the numbers directly and on the spot. In the end, our managers are behavioralists instead of numbers guys, and that's because we've learned that the numbers, while critically important, are the *result* of the behaviors we influence.

TURN EVERYDAY MISTAKES INTO LEARNING OPPORTUNITIES

Applauding positive behavior is great, but what happens when people get it wrong? How do you prevent your culture and your company from going off the rails without knee-jerk recourse to the kind of negativity and disempowerment that takes place when a typical command-and-control boss stands over you, makes you aware of your faults, and requires that you change or else?

The key is to reframe deficits or mistakes in a positive way: as learning opportunities. In the Feedback Loop, we ask people to tell us one thing they did well, but we also ask them to identify one thing they can enhance about their performance. Likewise, we alert them to one thing we think they could improve on as well. When a manager notices behavior in the moment that needs improvement, he or she will offer a short correction like "Move faster"; "Smile!"; "Let's seat that guest now."

We deliberately use the word "enhance" and not "do better"; "do better" implies that our team members did something wrong, and while we want to make team members more aware of areas where we'd like to see better behavior, we don't want them to dwell on the negative. "Perfect" behavior doesn't exist. No matter what level you're at, you can always up your game, so long as you keep a positive attitude. What's important is that employees become more mindful of their actions and of ways they can improve.

Many companies, upon providing feedback, say good things about a team member but then qualify it with a "but." "You're doing a great job leading people, *but* we wish you weren't so aggressive." "We love how much attention you pay to detail, *but* we wish you turned around your work assignments faster." We don't think of our feedback as "positive" and "negative" with a "but" in between. Rather, we think of both kinds of feedback as positive with an "and" in between. The point is to constantly affirm what people are already doing well and take that same positive energy to enhance other things that could be done even better. Because we're tracking performance so closely, we're also able to provide statements that are much more specific than those mentioned above. Instead of telling people we "wished they weren't so aggressive," we tell them, "We'd like to see you focus on using a softer tone of voice when you speak with the pizza makers you're coaching, and also, please give them enough time to make pizzas the right way before stepping in and doing it yourself." With this specific information, we're giving a limited, more manageable growth assignment to team members.

We also invite team members to speak first during feedback discussions, which allows us to see how aware teammates are of their behavior. It also increases knowledge retention since people tend to remember something better when they discover or uncover it themselves. Because team members know they will be asked about their behavior, this process fosters a habit of self-observation. We don't want team members to expect a manager to tell them what to do; we want them to naturally start a conversation like this on their own and by themselves, when no manager is present.

We see the benefits of this process with every shift, every day, every person. Cody was a seventeen-year-old pizza maker who started with us in 2009. To certify as a pizza maker, he needed to be able to make a pizza to spec within sixty seconds. In the beginning, he was doing many things well: putting the right amount of sausage on the pizza; always moving quickly to do his job efficiently; keeping his eyes up to anticipate what to do next; saying "please," "thank you," and "behind you" to people. But there were a few behaviors he needed to enhance: keeping his sausage pieces a uniform nickel size; putting sauce on the pizza efficiently; and putting the right amount of cheese on the pizza. After a shift, we'd point his attention to one of these things, and Cody, an enthusiastic learner, was diligent about working on it. Within only one shift, we had enhanced the specific behavior we identified, to the point where we were able to applaud him for doing it well. This freed him to begin working on another very specific behavior, and within six shifts over a period of one to two weeks, he became certified in his position, performing to support our culture as well as we could have hoped.

In addition to honing pizza-making skills, our feedback system benefitted Cody personally. This was only the second job he had ever had, and he was nervous. It didn't help matters that he came from a broken home in a low-income area of our community. After two weeks and one certification, Cody found his mojo. He was vibrant and interacting much more confidently with the team. In the end, Cody trained and certified in six positions, which qualified him for a dollar raise and the status of a red hat, or "pro." He also graduated at the top of his class and is now attending Marquette University on a full scholarship.

Chanti had just turned eighteen when she came to work for us in our Heart of House. She was a very small woman, "four foot eleven and a half," as she liked to tell us. Like Cody, she came from a broken home and was one of five or six children, several of whom had children of their own out of wedlock. When she walked through our big doors, she was already pregnant. Working toward her pizza-maker certification, she needed enhancement in many of the same skill areas as Cody. She too worked to up her game and achieved certification within two weeks. After taking a two-month leave to have her baby, she stepped back into an aggressive development track, always taking our enhancement suggestions seriously and implementing them quickly. Within a year, she had certified in nine positions, qualifying her for a black hat and about three dollars worth of raises over her starting rate. She had even certified in the most difficult position in our Heart of House, pizza puller, which required her to pull hot pizzas out of our four ovens, all of which were as tall as she was. And she went through our 300-level leadership training class, qualifying her to train others and participate in our profit-sharing program.

Today Chanti is a Heart of House team member and trainer. Her personal growth has been astounding. She takes charge, leading teams through an $8,000 shift, and her voice is among the loudest in our kitchen. Having discovered her passion, she's attending photography school, all the while continuing to work at Nick's. In five years, she plans to own her own photography business "and still work at Nick's," stating this goal with such confidence that I don't doubt for a minute she'll achieve it. "When I used to go out to different stores, I never used to talk with anybody," Chanti says. "Now I'm constantly saying, 'Have a great day' or, 'How is your weekend?' I'm confident enough to have conversations with people and just laugh." A person like Chanti could so easily have turned bitter in response to her life experiences. A job where she was constantly being told what she was doing wrong might make her feel this way. Giving her opportunities to improve herself has allowed us to help her be her best.

Although almost all of our team members have stories like this, a few aren't able to adjust to our tracking system. Because we monitor behavior so closely and consistently, we can quickly figure out when an individual isn't responding well to our suggested enhancements. The trainer and Operating Partner will then sit down with the team member and have a conversation about the specific behaviors that require course correction. They'll make it clear that if we aren't seeing performance enhancements during the next couple of shifts, then perhaps the job isn't a good fit. If the same problem shows up twice, we tell the team member that although we may like her, her competency in the skills we need doesn't match our company's performance criteria, and perhaps it would be better for her to find a position that more naturally complements her behavior. As Stephen Covey notes in his book *Speed of Trust*, we need to be able to trust both the character and competency of the individuals we hire. If we doubt a person's performance and need to double-check his work, it slows down the performance of the whole group. A good personality or strong character is not enough to remain part of the Nick's team.

This system of helping poorly performing team members out the door via coaching in the moment has several advantages. First, it allows us to save thousands of dollars on wages and unemployment benefits for an individual we eventually would have had to let go. It also sends an unspoken message to our team about how seriously we take high performance. The seventeen- and eighteen-year-olds who do make it see firsthand that the bar is high, and that we take very deliberate action when someone doesn't cut it. They understand that it's difficult to work at Nick's, which makes what they've already achieved seem that much sweeter and gives them the confidence to keep going. Meanwhile, those whom we've let go usually leave without any drama, since they understand that we aren't judging their character or abilities, just their performance.

PUTTING NUMBERS TO BEHAVIOR

If you're a traditional manager trained as a hardheaded numbers person, you might be skeptical of our qualitative methods. Well, let me reassure you: We like numbers, too. Since most companies don't quantitatively assess behavior, we've had to experiment with our own proprietary methods. For instance, to track how well servers are connecting with guests, we created a special form that captures how many guests request each individual server. As I'll describe in detail at the beginning of the next chapter, we put this data on a financial board and share it with our team members so that we can create public, peer-to-peer competition to get the most guest requests. As a result, we see servers discerning more of the things they're already doing to connect well with guests, and they're also pioneering new forms of unscripted behavior.

In assessing company performance, we leave empty space at the bottom of our financial boards so we can include quantitative metrics around behaviors we'd like to improve. Recently, our bus-sers began to rate our servers on how well they pre-bussed their tables (that is, cleared away a few of the dirty plates as they gave out checks and processed payments). These numbers went up on our financial boards, and you wouldn't believe how much better our servers got at pre-bussing. This result was especially remarkable when you consider that bussers are usually seen as below servers in a restaurant hierarchy. By letting bussers rate our servers, we sent an organizational message that hierarchy doesn't exist at Nick's, and that anybody in our company is in a position to rate the behav-ior of anyone else.

Another key behavior measure relates to guest comment cards. Like many restaurants, we distribute cards to our guests, asking them to rate their experience. We do this every six days, so that the day of the week is always changing and we can get a variable read on our quality. We have a profit-sharing program in place for all team members who complete 301, and servers and carry-out hosts in our pool get a share only if comment cards for their entire group are at least 99% positive. The card itself breaks down service to specific dimensions of behavior, includ-ing friendliness and whether the server checked back with the table quickly to ensure satisfaction. Knowing that extra cash is at stake, servers dig deep to perform these behaviors and deliver the Nick's experience. We also use these cards as an opportunity to celebrate desired behavior. When guests go out of their way to write a special note describing outstanding service, we post that publicly on our financial board, recognizing that this kind of behavior directly impacts our numbers.

It pays to be nimble when putting numbers to behavior. During 2008, we received a couple of complaints about mistakes with our carry-out orders. Items were missing, sandwiches were made wrong, and guests were upset. We started tracking how many consecutive orders in a row we could fill without a mistake. This encouraged teams to fill orders more meticulously and to check what was inside an order bag against the ticket. We discovered we were filling orders far more accurately than most restaurants, but we're still glad we made this effort. Instead of going 800 orders without a mistake, as we had been doing, we were able with some effort and healthy competition to jack that number up to 1,200. We even found a way to tweak our point-of-sale computer system to print out tickets in a way that reduces confusion and mistakes while improving efficiency. Our carry-out hosts began consciously repeating orders back to the guests before they even entered them into our system—all because we made an effort to monitor behavior with numbers.

BEHAVIOR ISN'T EVERYTHING

Just because we focus on tracking behaviors doesn't mean we miss out on what managers at most companies think about—the hard financial stuff. I would argue that an organization that's serious about its culture also goes further to deploy sophisticated financial tracking. Money is essential to any company, even one built around a strong nonfinancial purpose. External financial measurements turn out to be very much part of our internal culture, which is why we've included financial health as one of our core values.

Working closely with Rudy Miick, we've implemented financial tracking tools that the vast majority of companies in our industry don't have. In 2003, when I was still languishing in the depths of niceness, Rudy helped us tighten our fiscal reporting systems, especially as they related to purchasing, our biggest expense. One of the main reasons restaurants close is that they're inefficient in purchasing, keeping way too much inventory on hand. Typically, restaurants focus on simply keeping a stable inventory (that is, enough of every product on hand to avoid shortages). At the end of each month, the restaurant tallies the cost of goods sold to determine how it is performing on three prime costs: food, beverage, and labor. Makes sense, right? In fact, this system of purchasing and reporting is highly inefficient. Restaurants typically keep thousands of dollars of unused product on the shelf, a practice that sucks up available cash. And since they report these figures only once a month, they don't have an opportunity to reduce waste or improve sales. It's like doing an autopsy on a dead body: They amass data on what did happen, rather than project what will happen.

What we do instead is report our sales on a daily basis. Rudy helped us implement what's called a purchase-costing system, a process of analysis based on our forecasted sales and purchasing cycles (for example, we turn our cheese and meat inventories over two or three times a week). Every morning, we review what we're forecasting for both lunch and dinner sales. These numbers are based on budgets for the whole year, last year's sales for the same day, the weather forecast, events taking place in the community, and our sense of how we've trended over the past four weeks. Our Operating Partner produces a monthly forecast, but the manager for each day will take a look at it again, see what factors have changed, and make appropriate revisions. We also examine our previous day's and week's sales data relative to our costs in order to check whether we had excess inventory on hand. And we do this for food, beverage, and labor costs.

If we do have excess inventory on hand, we can use it up

by holding promotions—a special on fried mushrooms, a contest among servers to sell mozzarella sticks, a two-for-one drink special. By proactively driving sales, we're able to purchase more efficiently, which really helps us maximize financial performance. All this means more cash on hand that we aren't using to buy product we don't need.

Before our purchase-costing system, we struggled during the two weeks before and after Christmas. Knowing we're usually slow after Thanksgiving for a whole month, I would keep less product on hand, but inevitably kids would get out of school around Christmas, and we'd have a two-week surge, with sales jumping 20%. When we ran out of big items like sausage, cheese, or vegetables, I'd run to the grocery store and pay top dollar. Worst of all, the kids would go back to school in January, and with the resulting sales drop, I'd wind up with a lot of excess spoiled product. Like most restaurant managers, I wasn't analyzing what I needed to buy (that is, linking it to actual sales), nor was I analyzing it frequently enough (on a daily or weekly basis). I was always playing catch-up in what I was buying relative to demand. Under our new system, we forecast sales more accurately for each week and finely tune our purchase orders to reflect minute daily fluctuations in our demand. We keep on hand what we need, pay the best prices, and prevent ourselves from losing sales because we run out of product, even during periods when it's hard to predict extreme fluctuations in demand.

Aside from this costing system, we make our whole team in each restaurant aware of daily and shift-wise financial goals to a far greater extent than other restaurants I've seen. Before every lunch and dinner shift, we hold the usual pre-shift meeting. At most restaurants, the talk is about menu specials, wine pairings for the day, and the like. We talk about those things, but we spend most of our time talking about sales goals. We break these down into goals for selling specific items, such as appetizers and cocktails. Using a pre-shift form I developed years ago (see below), based on a form and concepts put forth by Jack Stack and Bo Burlingham in their book *The Game of Business*, we make sure managers cover the cultural and financial essentials, including sales goals, guest check average goals, and labor cost goals, as well as any events going on in the community that impact our sales results and any special events in the restaurant that may impact sales (all of these are incorporated below under "forecasting"). Even as our people are paying close attention to their behavior, they always—*always*—have the bottom line in mind. The point is not to focus on one at the expense of the other, but to constantly deepen our appreciation of the relationship between the two, and of the holistic entity that is a well-functioning business.

NICK'S PIZZA & PUB FISCAL HUDDLES

HUDDLE STRUCTURE

I.   Critical Number
II.   Forecasting
III.   Stake in the Game (What's in it for each of us)
IV.   Profit Sharing
V.   Accountability
    A. Line Item Owners = R.F.D. (report, forecast, deliver)
VI.   End with "Appreciation"*

....

* I borrowed this last step from Ari Weinzweig of the famous Zingerman's Deli in Ann Arbor, Michigan. I met Ari at a Games of Business conference. Since then, not only have I drawn inspiration from his leadership through workshops I have attended, including the Zingerman's Experience training program, but he has also become a friend.

RESPONSIBILITY ASSIGNED TO:

Line Item Owners	*Action: Update huddle numbers prior to meeting start time.*
Facilitator	*Set up meeting space, check-in, reinforcement, keep group on task.*
Timekeeper	*Start and stop on time.*
Note Taker	*Record action steps and distribute by the end of the day.*

BEHAVIOR AND THE BOTTOM LINE

Happily, our system for tracking behaviors leads directly to measurable financial improvements. In our Heart of House, we track sales per labor hour, a number that tells us how productive a person is per hour of sales. Companies can influence that number by telling people to work harder, or they can coach behaviors that support that number: moving fast from one task to another; performing a task efficiently; keeping your hands moving while you're talking and having fun with your teammates. Our managers know to coach specifically around these behaviors; the result is that, during slow times, when a team at a restaurant might ordinarily behave in a way that will lead to a dip in productivity (for example, hanging around chatting), our teams continue to work at the same pace, taking an opportunity to clean, break down boxes, or restock according to the operations cards they use as guides. Tracking behavior leads us to understanding the link between certain numbers and certain behaviors, which in turn leads to modeling and affirming good behavior, which in turn leads to more desirable behavior, which in turn leads to better numbers.

It's important to puzzle out links between behavior and financial results as fully as possible. Most companies explain big-picture numbers by tying them to other big-picture numbers; for instance, a manager might explain a drop in revenue by pointing to a wholesale decline in customer satisfaction. Not us. At one of our restaurants, our managers mentioned how bar sales had increased and how we wanted to replicate that at our other restaurant. Instead of going straight to a metric like customer satisfaction, we asked, "What are the behaviors leading to the increased bar sales?" Our Operating Partner Scott noticed that our bar guests were talking to one other, and that this was because our bartender, Mike, would take a step or two back when serving, engaging multiple guests in conversation with eye contact and arm movements. As guests formed friendships with other guests, they lingered longer, which led to higher bar sales—and also supported our purpose of creating community. We added this behavior to our 201 training for bartenders, on the "art" side, and when we noticed one of our barbacks (the guys who typically wash dishes in the back of the bar) not engaging in this way, we put in place a "science" element and devised a tracking exercise whereby our manager would check in with him hourly and ask him to list personal facts about three different guests. The result: Bar sales increased even more.

Tracking behavior builds on our business by influencing what guests and others in our community think of us and our people. Because our team members are working so hard to improve, and because they're employing tracking techniques such as Moments of Magic, they're behaving well even after they leave our restaurants. I hear it all the time in our community: "People who work at Nick's are really nice!" We've even begun using tracking as a marketing tool to spread positive energy around the

A sampling of the many Moment of Magic cards we post for everyone to see.

community. We give team members Moment of Magic cards to hand out to others in the community when they see positive, helpful, altruistic behavior that's consistent with the Nick's Experience; printed on the card is a coupon for a free appetizer. On a superficial level, we're giving prospective guests an incentive to try our restaurant while simultaneously empowering even the most junior team member to build sales. More deeply, we're showing the community that we care about behavior, are always watching, and are doing our best to celebrate behavioral victories, so that they become more frequent. Guess what? Our community appreciates the gesture! And they show their appreciation by becoming loyal guests.

This chapter has made a business case for tracking and celebrating the everyday behavioral victories we all experience on the job. Most managers sense that behavior directly affects performance, which is why companies adopt formal recognition and reward programs for employees. At Nick's, we don't need such programs, because recognition and reward are constantly happening at our company, with even better results. Organizations should go straight to their people—and to the culture—to help produce business goals rather than focusing on any one financial number. The way to do that is through influencing behavior.

Organizations that get as crazy as we are about observing behavior are likely to see the same results we've enjoyed: more on-purpose behavior, a stronger culture, a keenly motivated workforce, and industry-leading performance. Tracking, not hoping, is the perfect and necessary complement to trusting, and once you combine the two, great things will happen.

CHAPTER SEVEN
Become as Transparent as Possible

When I first decided to open a restaurant, everyone told me I was crazy to think I could trust hourly employees. Not only did people assume team members wouldn't care as much as I did, they claimed team members would undermine the business—stealing, slacking on the job, adopting an "us-against-the-man" attitude. I rejected this idea, but plenty of command-and-control companies don't, which is why they feel the need to micromanage. Unfortunately, as anyone who has ever labored under command and control knows, cynicism about your workforce risks becoming a self-fulfilling prophecy. If you don't trust your people, they won't trust you, and vice versa.

Command-and-control leadership proves especially damaging to companies when it comes to communications about business performance. Such companies hold information too close to the vest, leading individuals and layers of internal bureaucracy to respond in kind. Executives assume others are keeping secrets, so they spy on them—for example, using cameras or secret shoppers—and monitor their e-mails and Web usage. Teamwork suffers, trust disintegrates even further, and the culture corrodes from within. In my experience, these effects are only exacerbated when you're dealing with younger team members who tend to naturally feel cynical about authority and respond harshly when they perceive they're being lied to. As I like to say, Generation Y needs to know why.

At Nick's, we list "open and honest communication" as one of our explicit values and back up that value by sharing financial and human-resource information with team members. This includes being honest about budgets, actual sales and revenue results, and salaries. More fundamentally, we tackle challenges, difficulties, and embarrassing situations head-on by talking about them openly, with both team members and guests, using our Safe Space communication tool. It's true we don't practice 100% transparency. We don't share our food-cost percentage with guests, because those who lack information about the rest of our costs or knowledge about business operations would likely misunderstand this number and say, "Jeez, these guys are making so much profit." And of course, we don't share personal information about our team members because we respect everyone's privacy.

But when it comes to information that, if released, won't directly threaten the company's existence or otherwise conflict with the company's culture, we lay it all out there. In most cases, disclosure is consistent with our culture because it creates a sense of community that helps people feel they are working together. For instance, I've shared a lot about Nick's in this book because I want to help other organizations experience the results we have. I also believe that any heightened competition we might see would only prompt us to up our game. I encourage any business owner out there to put aside fears about sharing information, because chances are they're way overblown. The looser your boundaries, the better defined your culture can be and, paradoxically, the more cohesive your organization.

OPENING UP

Transparency at Nick's begins with the kind of information most companies find especially difficult to share: data about financial performance. Following management guru Jack Stack's Open Books approach, we present fiscal information to the team, using a financial board to post weekly results, including sales, costs, guest retention figures, customer comments, and a sales thermometer. We share this data at our fiscal meetings, which are open to all team members. The point of this isn't simply to allow team members to understand how the company is doing, but to permit us to huddle together and work through specific line items so that team members better understand how their jobs impact performance.

In weekly meetings, we use a 4x8 whiteboard to post line items on the profit-and-loss statement—things like dining room sales, bar sales, and carry-out sales, food cost, beverage cost, labor, etc. Team members own a line on that board for an entire four-week period. Tim, a red-hat cook in our Elgin restaurant, might have to report on beverage costs for the week, outlining what the budgeted cost was the previous week, what the actual cost was, the reasons behind any discrepancy between these numbers, and the forecast cost for the coming week. Then we have a group discussion about our performance, the factors contributing to it, and action steps we're going to take to influence results.

As dry as financial meetings may sound, we keep ours energetic and inspiring, with managers serving primarily to facilitate the process. "I love these huddles," one of our team members says. "To know exactly what needs work financially has been great. I love being able to have a hard-core brainstorming session

Our meeting table and, behind it, our financial board.

with the passionate people that attend. And it's great to have a voice in where we are going." Ben, one of our black-hat cooks, emphasizes the feeling of personal responsibility and connectedness to the company that comes with Open Books: "At our huddles, I feel as though I know I can make an impact on sales, guest experiences, and data. Also, I know precisely *how* I make an impact. I come away feeling that my daily work leads directly to fiscal success or failure at Nick's." Our manager Jen reports that "having huddles helps all team members become aware of what they can do to help. We can avoid the drama that comes when people make assumptions. Also, the huddles have become creative sales meetings, and we have come up with some great ideas!"

In addition to teaching our team members about the finances of our business, these meetings allow them to interact more effectively with guests, activity that leads to higher sales. Recently, we phased out the extremely popular half-price promotions we'd introduced to help our community deal with the 2007–2008 recession. We anticipated this move would upset many of our customers, and we were right. "How could you do this?" many asked. "You guys seem like you're making tons of money. Certainly you could afford it." Because we had announced the decision to our team, heard their concerns, and explained the financial logic behind what we were doing, they were able to inform guests that we had kept the promotions in place for two years but just couldn't sustain it financially any longer. "When I would first tell a guest about the change they would seem upset about it," server Natalie Levita remembers. "Then when I shared with them how we had given back $1.1 million to the community over the last two years, and how we were seeing our Friday, Saturday, and Sunday business cannibalized, they were appreciative." Some guests still stopped coming in, possibly because they couldn't afford to pay our full prices. But at least they had data on hand to understand our point of view, and they were less likely to feel resentful going forward. As one of our team members puts it, "Open Books allowed me to not make up any stories about where all the money was going; it kept everything real!"

The Open Books concept, as Stack outlines it, relates specifically to financial data, but we figure why stop there? At Nick's, we include other data related to human resources that most companies don't share. For example, at the team-member level, everyone knows everyone else's hourly wage, and thanks to our system of advancement (the hats: tan, red, and black; see Chapter Four), they know precisely what they and everyone else needs to do to advance. As a result, when sales take a dip during tough financial times, there's no need to tap-dance around the issue of reducing our hourly-wage workforce to meet our revenues; wage information is out there, so we can all talk through our situation and come up with a solution that team members understand. (We don't have as much discussion around the salaries of our executives because they are paid a budgeted fixed percentage of sales. What we talk about isn't about what each manager is making but rather whether a group's cost percentage is coming in as budgeted, and if not, why not.)

You're probably wondering if people in the company know my salary. Actually, they do. Anybody who wants to can look it up on the full profit-and-loss statement hanging on the financial board. I will admit it wasn't easy at first to provide that information to the entire company, and initially I thought I could get away without disclosing it since people would just say, "Well, he's the boss." Then I caught myself. If ever there was a time to send a strong message about our values, to do the unexpected and garner trust from the organization in return, this was it. I not only shared my salary, but I acknowledged that it was higher than anyone else's, and that if at any time people didn't feel I was earning my keep, they should let me know immediately. This hasn't happened yet, but I did impress our team with how seriously I regard transparency and my willingness to be held to the same standards as everyone else.

Open and honest communication affects our dealings with the public, too. Our restaurants have open kitchens that allow customers to watch their pizzas being made, and we welcome executives from other companies to experience our 301 training. Everything about our guest experience conveys transparency, from the servers and hosts who let their authentic selves hang out, to the homey décor and peanuts on the floor that make guests feel they can relax, to the layout that affords nearly all tables a view of the wide-open common area. As people in our

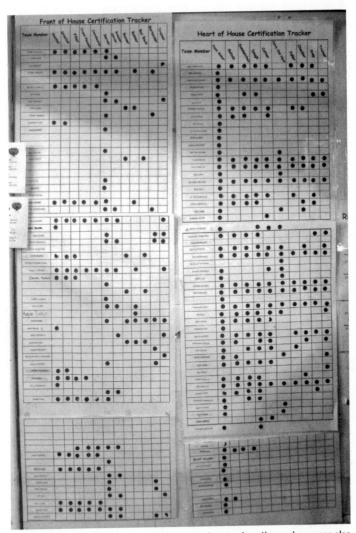

Our certification tracking board, so that everyone knows where they and everyone else stand.

Benefit Costing Sheet

Medical Insurance: Non-Manager Team Member Only

	MONTHLY COST	NICK'S PAYS	TEAM MEM-BER PAYS	PER PAY-CHECK
BASE PLAN	$265.72	$132.86	$132.86	$61.32
BUY UP OPTION #1	$296.02	$132.86	$163.16	$75.30
BUY UP OPTION #2	$370.79	$132.86	$237.93	$109.81

Medical Insurance: Non-Manager Team Member + Spouse

	MONTHLY COST	NICK'S PAYS	TEAM MEM-BER PAYS	PER PAY-CHECK
BASE PLAN	$584.57	$132.86	$451.71	$208.48
BUY UP OPTION #1	$651.25	$132.86	$518.39	$239.26
BUY UP OPTION #2	$826.77	$132.86	$682.87	$315.17

Medical Insurance: Non-Manager Team Member + Children

	MONTHLY COST	NICK'S PAYS	TEAM MEM-BER PAYS	PER PAY-CHECK
BASE PLAN	$504.86	$132.86	$372.00	$171.69
BUY UP OPTION #1	$562.45	$132.86	$429.59	$198.27
BUY UP OPTION #2	$704.50	$132.86	$571.64	$263.83

Medical Insurance: Non-Manager Team Member + Family

	MONTHLY COST	NICK'S PAYS	TEAM MEM-BER PAYS	PER PAY-CHECK
BASE PLAN	$823.72	$132.86	$690.06	$318.49
BUY UP OPTION #1	$917.67	$132.86	$784.81	$362.22
BUY UP OPTION #2	$1149.45	$132.86	$1,016.59	$469.20

Dental Insurance: Non-Manager Team Member

TEAM MEMBER MONTHLY/PER PAYCHECK	TM + SPOUSE MONTHLY/PER PAYCHECK	TM + CHILD MONTHLY/PER PAYCHECK	TM + FAMILY MONTHLY/PER PAYCHECK
$23.12 / $10.67	$45.03 / $20.78	$58.43 / $26.97	$80.34 / $37.08

Vision: Non-Manager Team Member

TEAM MEMBER MONTHLY/PER PAYCHECK	TM + SPOUSE MONTHLY/PER PAYCHECK	TM + CHILD MONTHLY/PER PAYCHECK	TM + FAMILY MONTHLY/PER PAYCHECK
$6.38 / $2.94	$12.11 / $5.59	$12.76 / $5.89	$18.50 / $8.54

Benefit Costing Sheet

Medical Insurance: Manager Only

	MONTHLY COST	NICK'S PAYS	TEAM MEMBER PAYS	PER PAYCHECK
BASE PLAN	$265.72	$212.58	$52.94	$24.43
BUY UP OPTION #1	$296.02	$212.58	$83.44	$38.51
BUY UP OPTION #2	$370.79	$212.58	$158.21	$73.02

Medical Insurance: Manager + Spouse

	MONTHLY COST	NICK'S PAYS	TEAM MEMBER PAYS	PER PAYCHECK
BASE PLAN	$584.57	$212.58	$371.99	$171.69
BUY UP OPTION #1	$651.25	$212.58	$438.67	$202.46
BUY UP OPTION #2	$815.73	$212.58	$603.15	$278.38

Medical Insurance: Manager + Children

	MONTHLY COST	NICK'S PAYS	TEAM MEM-BER PAYS	PER PAY-CHECK
BASE PLAN	$504.86	$212.58	$292.18	$134.85
BUY UP OPTION #1	$562.45	$212.58	$349.87	$161.48
BUY UP OPTION #2	$704.50	$212.58	$491.92	$227.04

Medical Insurance: Manager + Family

	MONTHLY COST	NICK'S PAYS	TEAM MEM-BER PAYS	PER PAY-CHECK
BASE PLAN	$823.72	$212.58	$611.14	$282.06
BUY UP OPTION #1	$917.67	$212.58	$705.09	$325.42
BUY UP OPTION #2	$1,149.45	$212.58	$936.87	$432.40

Dental Insurance: Manager

TEAM MEMBER MONTHLY/PER PAYCHECK	TM + SPOUSE MONTHLY/PER PAYCHECK	TM + CHILD MONTHLY/PER PAYCHECK	TM + FAMILY MONTHLY/PER PAYCHECK
$23.12 / $10.67	$45.03 / $20.78	$58.43 / $26.97	$80.34 / $37.08

Vision: Manager

TEAM MEMBER MONTHLY/PER PAYCHECK	TM + SPOUSE MONTHLY/PER PAYCHECK	TM + CHILD MONTHLY/PER PAYCHECK	TM + FAMILY MONTHLY/PER PAYCHECK
$6.38 / $2.94	$12.11 / $5.59	$12.76 / $5.89	$18.50 / $8.54

Our benefits costs, outlined for everyone to see.

communities recognize, Nick's is the kind of place where you don't have to put on airs or cultivate an image. What you see is what you get, down to the rough-hewn beams and the huge stone fireplaces.

Because we value transparency, we do virtually no advertising. Advertising erects a barrier between your company and the general public, who know it's nothing more than a mask—a projection of what you *want* people to think you look like, not what you actually are. At Nick's, we're always trying to take off the mask and break down boundaries. We're behaving authentically, so our marketing task is simply to help the world become more aware of what we're actually doing. Over the years, I've hired marketing professionals, but they always wanted to do flyers, coupons, direct mail, and other kinds of advertising. That's not our brand. Maybe that's Domino's Pizza, but it's not us. We're about purpose and values, and we want everything in our company—including our communications—to reflect that in a transparent way.

A great tool for engaging transparently with the public is social media. Since our guests are on Facebook and Twitter, we've asked our team to be on Facebook and Twitter, too. We don't tell our people what to say but ask them to share what's new and exciting in our company and what our challenges are. Our sole requirement: Use Safe Space practices while talking about us (that is, check the data, use "I" statements, etc.) We don't mind critical or negative statements about Nick's, so long as we can achieve the same level of discourse outside the company as exists inside the company. More companies today are moving toward social media, and I applaud that because it means they will be held accountable by everyone who is part of the conversation.

It's wonderful how far the boundary between the inside and the outside of a company can recede thanks to social media. In 2011, as the economy was rebounding from a brutal recession, I posted on Facebook saying that we had had a tough January and February and that our weekend sales had dropped. I asked guests: What would they do if they were us to bring in more sales? Some two dozen people left comments, and we said we'd consider their suggestions. In the end, we wound up introducing a different promotion each day of the week, recognizing that people in our community needed help financially if they were to dine out. This post got almost 6,000 hits. Another nineteen people commented on it. "Nick rocks!" one person said. "You guys set examples other businesses should follow. Things are not great yet. I hate to see that some businesses think 'happy days are here again' and make moves that are not customer-centric." In my mind, the best part about this communication was that it showed we respected our guests enough to give them a voice in what we were doing and then acted in a way that served their needs, not just the company's. I wish more consumer-facing companies would do that.

Some companies pursue social media as part of a formal marketing strategy. But we don't develop a strategy around marketing; we simply communicate the truth about what we're doing and let the strategy take care of itself. Even our routine marketing research serves as an opportunity for transparency. Whereas other companies may hire secret shoppers (third parties hired by management to pretend to be customers and report back on the customer experience and any employee screwups), we have our own team members come in for a free dinner so they can savor the Nick's Experience from the customer's point of view and provide on-the-spot feedback for improvement. Our marketing research is an extension of the friendly and supportive coaching we provide for one another every day. It builds bonds of trust rather than tears them down, which, after all, is the real objective of any marketing effort.

NAMING AND SOLVING PROBLEMS

Every company has problems, and while it's easy for executives to keep them under wraps, usually out of fear, they do themselves a disservice when they don't address problems openly. Even a company as seemingly invincible as Apple was guilty of this by refusing to comment on Steve Jobs's health problems, although they were obvious to anyone who had been paying attention for the last couple of years before his death. By failing to offer information, the company was doing several things: It was fueling rumors and speculation; it was missing an opportunity to build trusting relationships with members of the community; and it was missing out on all the ideas, help, and good wishes members of the community might have extended to Jobs, his family, and the company. Customers who might have felt goodwill toward the company and identified with Jobs's personal struggle instead were forced to make of it whatever they could, most likely assuming the worst. The company communicated that it had something to hide—a reality so terrible it dared not speak of it—and everyone naturally wondered, what else weren't they telling us?

At Nick's, we look for opportunities to reframe bad news, conflict, and criticism as learning opportunities. In the middle of the Facebook discussion described above, one guest commented: "Quit skimping on cheese on your pizzas. I'm going to start ordering pizza from other places." I wrote back within ten minutes and said, "You've got it, Shawn! Nine ounces of mozzarella made with real milk is a recipe for every pizza for the past thirty-five years. If you didn't get that, come in and see me, and I will make it right for you." In offering this response, I not only show a disgruntled guest that I care, but also communicate to potential guests that they're going to receive the same treatment. We're not afraid of critical feedback from guests, because instead of letting it hurt us, we use it as an opportunity to show guests just how much we respect them and their opinions. I have reviews from the Web site Yelp sent directly to my personal e-mail; that way, I can read them and respond in a truthful way almost instantly.

We aggressively unearth and solve problems inside our company as well. To make conflict and negativity less scary for people, we introduce new team members to the Moose in the Room concept on the very first day, and we remind them of it constantly by displaying a giant stuffed moose head above our fireplace. In a restaurant environment, perhaps the most common Moose is underperformance on the part of a team member— a pizza maker moving too slowly, for example, or a server failing to pre-bus her tables. Many team members are reluctant to point out poor performance, since they don't want to create conflict with someone they work with everyday and probably like as a person. We circumvent this problem by charging managers and trainers with recognizing when poor performance has persisted and become a theme. A sure sign is when a team begins avoiding the poor performer. Observing that, our trainers come in and say, "Wait a second. I'm noticing that we're having conversations about that person when they're not around, or we're starting to change our behavior because that person isn't performing. That's a Moose!"

A dating relationship in the workplace can also easily become a Moose. We used to have a "no dating" provision in our handbook, but then we realized that inevitably some team members would want to date one another, and the policy was unintentionally creating secrecy and a whole herd of Moose. Because of Safe Space, these issues now resolve themselves. Once, we had a manager-in-training, Jim, who had begun dating one of the hosts. I asked him how this would affect his performance on the job.

"I don't know," he replied. "Probably it won't make much of a difference. And Nick, I can't stop who I like or am attracted to."

"You're right," I said. "You sure can't stop who you're attracted to. But if you date someone who reports to you, you'll lose the respect of the rest of the host team, who will always be wondering if you're playing favorites. They'll always have their own Moose. How are you going to hold team members accountable for performance?"

Jim gave me a long look. "I hadn't thought of that."

I helped define what the options were for our lovelorn manager, and how they related to the purpose and values underlying our culture. He could either dissolve the relationship or work in our other restaurant, which was farther from his home. He decided to keep his girlfriend and move to the other location. Mindful of the need for transparency in most situations, we came in and promptly named the Moose, then did something about it before it damaged performance. In keeping with Trust and Track, I didn't simply tell Jim what to do; I gave him two choices and empowered him to decide for himself.

We encourage even our youngest team members to raise issues about those to whom they report. On one occasion, a twenty-year-old pizza puller named Kyle and I were talking in the Heart of House, and he told me that my back was facing the carry-out counter. This was an obvious error, as we teach all of our team members to stand face-to-face with guests so as to welcome them properly. "Wow, Kyle, you're right," I responded. "I didn't even realize I was doing it." I changed my position and came away from the encounter really happy with our Safe Space tool. Because our team members are so used to speaking their minds without fear of reprisal, a relative newbie like Kyle (he'd been with us for about a year) didn't hesitate to coach the owner. Now I could coach Kyle to use his awareness and communications skills more often with his team to raise their performance, too.

Our managers and I can't just sit around and wait for people like Kyle to point out improvement opportunities; we have to push ourselves to identify difficult problems up front, modeling behavior for everyone else and tackling problems early and aggressively. During the writing of this book, we had a meeting about our Mayor Pizza Making Showdown, a promotional event we were holding with the mayors of our town and a neighboring one. Everybody was assigned action steps to prepare for the big event, and mine was to consult with my brother's company to build a stage. It was such a key task that I didn't write it down, thinking, "How can I forget about the stage?" An hour and a half before the event, one of my managers said, "Nick, what are you doing about the stage?"

"Holy cow," I said, "I totally forgot."

A couple of team members and I ran across the street, obtained some plywood, and in a half hour used some racks in the basement to build a stage. At the end of the night, when we did our post-shift meeting and talked about the things that went well with the event and the things we had to enhance, nobody said anything about me forgetting something as big as the stage. Afterward, I asked our manager Jenny, "How come you're not holding me accountable about something as important as the stage? That's a big mistake; I really screwed up. Do you feel uncomfortable?"

She said, "Yeah, you're right, that's a big deal, and I do have to know that you're not going to make that mistake again. I assumed that you would do something different so it wouldn't happen again, but I don't know that for sure, so what *are* you going to do differently?"

It's critical for those of us in charge of businesses to open ourselves up to feedback and make ourselves vulnerable. When we do, the benefits can be huge. Consider the departure of Barry, whom I had hired as an Operating Partner with the idea of giving him more responsibility as our business expanded. Rudy thought we needed someone who was more of a systems thinker and had more experience with multiple restaurants. Barry fit the bill and was a great values match with us. He had worked at a number of large fast-casual restaurant chains and brought great sophistication into our company. From the moment he came onboard, he added structure to what we were doing, helping us develop systems around employee handbooks, our 201 training, our interview process, and our operations cards. Plus he was very well-liked, had high energy, and in general was a nice guy.

Unfortunately, things went south in 2008 when a planned expansion of our operations fell through (see Chapter Eight), and Barry had to return to strictly an Operating Partner role. Our revenues had a hard time sustaining his salary, and our overhead ballooned to 12–14% of revenues, when it should have been 6–8%. In keeping with our transparency ethic, I brought Barry into discussions about our situation, and we devised a plan to bring our overhead percentage in line by building up a catering business over the next year. As it turned out, the catering business didn't materialize. Meanwhile, as an Operating Partner of our second restaurant, Barry knew how to manage a profit-and-loss statement, but he wasn't effective when it came to inspiring the team as a coach. For the salary he was getting— double what our normal managers received—he needed to perform at a much higher level, and he needed to deliver better sales results. Jenny, a manager at the time, was starting to develop into an even stronger performer than Barry, so I decided to make her Operating Partner of our second restaurant. There just wasn't room for Barry any longer.

During this time, Barry and I were talking daily or weekly about the poor performance of the catering business. He was doing his best to improve the situation, but since he was so stressed out under the pressure, he wound up just creating more stress for the team around him. I waited and waited to do something, hoping that things would turn around in catering, but by October 2010, things hadn't improved, and I finally let Barry go. He was disappointed, but thanks to the transparency of our operations, not surprised. As he told me, "I believe in Nick's so much that the company's success is more important to me than my job. So let's do what we have to do. This won't be easy since I don't want to leave, but I also realize I need to."

Next I faced the challenge of letting our teams know. I broke the news to the company in a series of pre-shift meetings, as we always do whenever a team member leaves. As I told our team, "We need to keep our overhead percentage down relative to the amount of sales we're doing, and Barry was brought on to get us to five restaurants. If that progress is going to be stalled for some time, and we're not able to increase sales enough, then Barry isn't of value for us." Barry and I had worked together for seven years by this point, and he was as much a brother and a friend as he was a partner. We both had the same intentions, values, and perspective on the business. With him gone, I felt much more alone in the company. And I felt like I was also admitting my own failure. I hadn't been able to keep our relationship together, and I also hadn't been growing the company at the pace I'd wanted. I was quite nervous about telling the team, since I was concerned they would start to think that our company was falling apart. But I had the conversation anyway, mindful of our values and of Safe Space. We needed to be transparent about having a key leader in our company move on. It was a big deal.

As it turned out, breaking the news was easier than I'd thought. A couple of people were really sad, but others expressed concern about me personally and how I was doing. Team members told me, "This is the move we've been needing to make for a while now" and "We believe in our team." One said, "I've learned a great deal from Barry, but this is the best we can do, since he's not being as effective as before. We need to inspire our team and have them excited about being here." Over the next days and weeks, our teams drew tighter than ever. The speed with which our company moved seemed to increase. We had our weekly huddles without Barry about our fiscal numbers, and in those conversations our Operating Partners Jenny and Scott were far more proactive about making changes and improvements. Because people had had a chance to express their reaction to Barry's departure, we saw little bad blood and few doubts; people could quickly put the situation behind them and move our company ahead. This whole episode, while painful in the moment, didn't leave anyone wondering about what we were doing, why, and how people were feeling. Our company just came bouncing right back.

TRANSPARENCY AND COMMUNITY

People who hear about my business always ask me how we're able to take a bunch of energetic, hormone-charged teens and twenty-somethings and make a loyal, focused, winning team out of them. This, after all, is the same cohort that generates all those sad headlines about cliques, bullying, and violence in the schools. As I've related all along in this book, the key is to create a true *learning community*—a school masquerading as a restaurant—that engages young adults around self-development and serving a higher purpose. Specific actions and processes based on trust all help systematize and solidify this community, but we've found transparency in communication to be especially important, for a number of reasons.

First, transparency helps minimize the drama that almost always destroys communal feelings as well as any kind of real learning experience. As anyone who interacts with teens on a regular basis knows, they are notoriously prone to drama, with the attendant backbiting, blaming, bullying, gossip, and animosity. Recognizing that one of the chief sources of drama is poor communication, we circumvent the nastiness by getting the entire team focused collectively on speaking their truth about a problem, determining what's going wrong, and deciding what needs to happen to get performance back on track. Safe Space, in particular, takes all the wasted energy injected into drama and allows us to funnel it directly into team behavior. We've minimized drama to the point where, as we saw in Chapter Five, we have young team members who appreciate how their coaches live without drama and approach us asking how they can do so as well.

Transparency also fosters a learning community by inviting outsiders in to ask questions. Jill, a member of our accounting team, came to us from Arthur Andersen, the large corporate accounting firm that eventually folded after the Enron scandal. Initially, she was skeptical about our culture of learning; she'd heard a lot of talk about culture in her old job, but when push came to shove, she'd always found that it was just talk. Colleagues backstabbed one another, you were never really free to speak up and say what you felt, and you never felt comfortable asking questions. "If you wanted to learn something, you couldn't, because you always felt like you were going to offend someone or look stupid."

After some months at Nick's, Jill realized that people really were able to speak up. "The honesty around here allows someone like me the chance to admit when I don't understand or know something, and that's allowed me to really feel comfortable learning with my teammates, like we're all in this together. I didn't know anything about a restaurant at first, but my questions were always accepted. And when you get that, you feel like asking more, and it spirals up. Now I'm reviewing the profit-and-loss statements, and when I have questions at a deep level that can be kind of touchy, I can ask them. I know we can talk about it without it being an awkward situation."

Transparency also integrates team members into our system of in-the-moment learning, allowing them to feel comfortable coaching others and being coached. It gives young adults in particular a greater sense of empowerment and belonging in the community by enabling bottom-up coaching. For instance, Christy, one of our young servers, once had to interrupt a manager's meeting to get a swipe card she needed so that other servers could check out on the computer after their shifts. Because she felt so comfortable offering feedback in the moment, she later approached her manager, James, and asked him to let her know in the future when he would be in the meeting and also to leave the swipe card outside so she wouldn't need to barge in and interrupt. "Really what I was doing was coaching my manager on how to communicate more effectively. He took the coaching very well and said that I was right; he had failed to communicate well. That solved the problem. So I learned right then and there how to be an effective coach, and I also got the feeling of being a respected member of a group of people who were all interested in learning and helping others to learn."

In so many other companies, managers never learn much about their deficiencies in dealing with subordinates; all they have, in essence, are generic 360-degree surveys. In our culture, everybody learns, and everybody feels empowered to teach, simply because they know it's okay to say what's on their minds in the service of learning.

Our practices of transparency create bonds by implicitly inviting people to make honest mistakes in front of other community members. Our trainers are expected to be experts in open and honest communication about performance miscues. As one of them relates, "We need honest communication in order to help people improve and learn. Otherwise, people are going to start censoring themselves and closing themselves off from others. We're trained specifically to feel comfortable talking to other people about their mistakes. Little by little, you do see them loosen up and accept that they make mistakes, and that it's okay, because we're all here as partners and friends. You see them embrace the team and themselves. The community spirit is awesome."

This attitude of extreme openness on the part of our managers makes a strong impression on younger team members. Remember Justin from Chapter Four, the young man whose mother had been sent to prison? We initially hired him and then fired him when he made a mistake. He apologized to his manager, and we decided to give him a second chance. Upon re-entering our company, he stood up in the middle of a pre-shift meeting, surrounded by older team members, and publicly apologized for his mistake. As our manager Scott notes, "You don't get that very often. You don't get a kid who's going to actually want to admit to everyone that he made a mistake. He just stood up and said that he'd been wrong, that he was getting a second chance, and that he wasn't going to blow it. Him standing up like that was really something." This gesture reflected great courage and maturity on Justin's part, but it also reflected his trust in our community, the sense that he belonged and would be accepted here as a seeker of high performance, even and especially with his flaws in full view.

Perhaps the deepest way transparency facilitates entrance into our learning community is the encouragement it gives people to be honest with *themselves.* One of our managers, Amy, has acknowledged to others that she tends to offer servers too much help as they run food from the food window to the tables rather than supporting them to do their jobs on their own. As one of her reports remarked, "Her stating that will help improve both me and the team. I've always felt comfortable identifying things she could work on even though she's my boss. It helps me coach her more easily, and it also prompts me to recognize my own weaknesses. When you have people modeling honesty and truth, and when you see them growing, you want to do that, too."

Omar, another manager, went away to a retreat at the Gestalt

Institute and returned with an epiphany: To shine on the job, he needed to own up to his mistakes in the moment far more than he did, so that team members could learn from his example and therefore feel comfortable giving him the performance feedback he needed. Omar had originally thought he needed to model not merely high performance but *perfect* performance to the team. He learned a vital lesson: High performance doesn't preclude presenting your own humanness for all to see.

FROM A BOY TO A SPONGE

As we've seen in this chapter, something as simple and natural as open and honest communication has the power to create a culture of trust that in turn gives rise internally to a learning community. Our practice of transparency is so powerful that it begets better communication and an increasingly greater sense of community, even beyond the walls of our restaurants. That's right, we've started to see our young team members take practices like Safe Space and share them with friends and family, a behavior that both improves the surrounding community and creates favorable impressions of Nick's. One of our black-hat cooks (soon to be a manager) describes how he has applied Safe Space to help nourish a business partnership with his close friend:

> My friend Brian and I have known each other for seven years. We have the ability to work side by side silently for hours. One challenge I am running into with Brian is getting him to be his own teacher. Brian and I plan to start a business once our finances support that idea. The challenge I am struggling with is to get Brian to be a

Learner. I have become a Learner because of my training at Nick's, and I need Brian to activate his own learning. What I have started to do is have conversations around why learning is important for me, all the while using the tools that I know. I'm slowly beginning to coach Brian on a few language pieces of Safe Space in order to cultivate a culture open to coaching between the two of us. It's been working pretty well so far, and Brian too has come to appreciate what Nick's is all about.

On a broader level, by encouraging people to believe in the company, we're creating fertile soil for marketing relationships to take root. When we opened our second restaurant in 2005, many people in the community viewed our fund-raising programs with suspicion. They just couldn't believe that we were actually giving 15% of proceeds back to the community. Then the Parents-Teachers Organization from a South Elgin grade school held a fund-raiser at Nick's. We kept all the receipts and added them up at the end of the night. Within ten days, we shared the sales numbers and gave the PTO a check for the proceeds. Only when people saw that we were open about the sales we generated and the checks we cashed for them did they start to participate.

There are so many paradoxes that arise around transparency. By showing our weaknesses, we actually build *stronger* relationships. By letting our guard down, we actually reduce the need to protect ourselves in the first place. Finally, by admitting to others how much we have to learn, we actually improve our capacity to learn.

One of our team members expresses this last point in a way

that warms my heart and affirms so much of what we're trying to do at Nick's: "Thanks to the communication here, I feel informed and included. I have a voice, and I now move through each day with learning and growing in my mind. I have graduated from a boy to a sponge."

CHAPTER EIGHT
Become a Cultural Warrior

As successful as Nick's has been at creating both a high-performance culture and a learning community, these ideals are incredibly difficult to maintain. The truth is, it would be much easier to aim for mediocrity and accept uninspired service, lackluster employees, and cynical managers. But if we did that, we'd be like many other pizza restaurants and the last thing the world needs. At Nick's we choose to remain vigilant about our culture, constantly battling our ingrained human tendencies—laziness, fear of the unknown, a desire to avoid uncomfortable or confusing situations—in order to deliver on our purpose. Yet even with the tools and processes presented in this book and the herculean efforts of our team members, ingrained tendencies have a way of creeping back in, diluting the culture, and sapping performance. As leader, I alone am responsible for ensuring that this doesn't happen; if I drop the ball, nobody else is in a position to step up. Authentic leadership is a 24/7 job, and leaders must remember that culture is a calling, not simply an effective management approach.

In their book *Spirit of the Dancing Warrior*, Jerry Lynch and Chungliang Al Huang describe the spiritual warrior as a person who accepts sacrifice, responsibility, and drive; who works hard even when others aren't looking; who welcomes opponents as partners; and who has become "comfortable with being uncomfortable." As a final principle for building high-performance culture, this chapter urges leaders to think of themselves as *cultural* warriors—practicing the discipline of the culture more completely than anyone else; innovating and enhancing the tools, systems, and practices; overseeing and modeling the coaching functions in the company; safeguarding the finances in support of the culture; and finding ways to stay positive and energized. While we've spent much of this book discussing the first three duties of the cultural warrior, the last two, as we'll see, are equally important.

You can't get the best results by just applying my message to your organization and forgetting about it. Of course, you shouldn't micromanage your business, but as a cultural warrior you do need to remain more fully engaged and committed to your own development and to that of the organization than founders, owners, presidents, and CEOs usually are. Cultural warriors are not just cultural experts; they're guides, coaches, visionaries, even gurus. If you can live up to these functions while never forgetting the basics of your business, you'll not only build a sustainable enterprise; you'll realize immense satisfaction and profound happiness. Like everyone else in your organization, you'll discover and rediscover that your work is so much more than just a job.

THE HOUSEHOLDER'S JOURNEY

The first and most fundamental dimension of the cultural warrior's role is cultivation of intense personal focus and discipline around the culture. Every moment I'm at work, whether I'm walking the dining room floor or sitting in the back office, I make sure I embody the values of growth and self-improvement I'm trying to instill in our team. I may no longer seek to become an expert pizza puller or waiter, but I do want to become a better author, financial manager, strategic thinker, and coach. And no matter what I'm working on, I pay attention to how even my smallest action reinforces our values and enhances what we provide our guests. Thanks to years of practice, my language, my tone, and my body language all align with our purpose in a nanosecond, and I'm now able to deploy tools like Safe Space and Karpman's Drama Triangle without even realizing it. Yet room for growth always exists. Just as each day is an opportunity for our team members to be observed and evaluated, so too it is for me, and I go through my day mindful that anyone on our team can and will deploy Safe Space in order to celebrate or correct my behaviors.

A few months ago, I was conducting a business meeting at one of our dining tables when a guest asked me for information about our charity-events programming. Since I was busy, I asked one of our hosts, Sammi, to help the guest. Sammi was in the process of training a new seater (a host who seats guests when their table is ready), and to her my tone of voice and body language felt too assertive. I was barking out an order, she thought, rather than kindly asking her to do something. She became upset and asked her manager, Amy, if we could have a Safe Space conversation. During the conversation, I realized I needed to work harder not on what I was saying, but on nonverbal cues that communicated hardness and aggressiveness. In small ways like this, my team helps me live out the Nick's culture ever more completely, and for that I am grateful. They know that just like all the Nick's team members, I am perpetually focusing my energies on growing and learning.

The cultural warrior's commitment to self-improvement and mindfulness may begin at work, but it hardly ends there. I can't emphasize enough how much I've internalized the discipline of pursuing the Nick's purpose. Nick's values are *my* values, and I strive to act on them in my daily life. When I walk around town on my own time, I find myself greeting everyone I see, including strangers, within five steps. When I make personal decisions as a consumer, I deploy our "Issue—Purpose & Values—Solution" tool, asking myself, "How is this purchase a values match for us?" and considering factors such as whether a particular brand gives back to the community or treats its employees well.

Recently I ended a gym membership after a yearlong stint. It was a perfectly adequate facility in terms of what most people look for in a gym—affordable, good equipment, etc. But none of the staff smiled at me, nor did they greet me or make eye contact when I brought back my towel or the key for my locker. Once when I lost my key and asked for help, no one seemed interested in helping me. I was appalled at the bad customer service, and I thought, "How can I keep going to a health club that isn't taking care of its clients? What message does that send about how Nick's perceives customer service? How does that serve our purpose and values?" The last straw came when I forgot my membership card for the first time in a year, and the attendant pointed to a sign on his desk that read, "You don't have your card, we're not going to help you." This company had systematically embraced a philosophy of carelessness and self-aggrandizement—the exact opposite of our emphasis on service to the community. I concluded that it had no place in my life.

I constantly deploy our coaching processes, communication tools, and Trust and Track approach as a parent, too. My three kids are older now; my youngest, Danny, is finishing up high school. For years, I've steered their behavior by abandoning the policeman role that punished them for doing something wrong and instead opted to recognize them for doing something right. Rather than wait for them to become restless and misbehave at the dinner table, I'd take the initiative and applaud them at times when they were sitting quietly and eating their dinner. When my kids got their report cards, I would make a point of noticing the good grades first. Then I'd say, "What are you going to do to get this D up with the other grades?"

I've found Safe Space especially valuable. Often when I bring home dinner, my son Danny is crabby and complains about the food and school. In the old days, I responded to his emotion in kind, yelling, "Don't talk to me that way!" These days I use "I" statements, track data, and pay attention to his body language in addition to his words. "Seems like you're a little cranky," I say. "I can tell you're hungry. Would you like to eat before talking more?" A smirk forms on his face, and he says, "Yeah, let me eat a little bit." After three or four minutes, we're having a nice conversation.

When my daughter, Michelle, was a teenager, she hung around with a group of girls who were drinking, smoking, staying out late, and dressing in a grungy way. Her mother, my ex-wife, confronted Michelle angrily, making harsh judgments about her friends and Michelle's own actions. "Damn it, Michelle," she'd say, "you can't hang around those girls. They are nothing but trouble." Although I normally respected her parenting style, I took a different approach here, tracking what was happening in Michelle's life, asking questions, and paying close attention to the subjective meaning I was creating. On one occasion, I asked Michelle to tell me the one thing about her friend Amy that she felt most connected the two of them. Hearing her response, I said, "So based on what you've shared with me, have you noticed that your friends seem to need you, and that you're playing the role of rescuer in their lives, bailing them out when they drink too much or smoke weed?" I wasn't judging Michelle, just raising her awareness by tracking data and asking her if she was paying attention to the same thing. I interacted with her just as I do with anyone at Nick's, and I monitored my own behavior during the encounter, realigning myself whenever I caught myself becoming emotional.

One night, Michelle's friends were out drinking in a car. The cops came, and her friends fled the scene, not knowing what to do. They called Michelle, and she snuck out in the middle of the night, picked them up, and snuck them back into our house through an open window. When I caught them in the living room, I didn't rant and rave but instead helped my daughter take care of one of the girls, who was still drunk. The next day, after Michelle's friends had left, I asked Michelle: "Are you noticing a trend here? Your friends are misbehaving, and you're playing the rescuer. Have you considered that this choice will cause people to write you off as part of that group? Have you thought about how you might not be taking care of your own life if you're constantly taking care of other people and they're not learning from the experience?" After the previous conversations we'd had, and with the actual data clearer than ever, my daughter finally got the message. She didn't make better decisions overnight, but she did improve her grades that year and got herself into a good college. Best of all, our relationship stayed warm and positive.

Disciplining ourselves to align our every act with our culture is not easy, especially in stressful situations. To stay focused, I recommend practicing other disciplines that link body, mind, and soul. I spend time alone each day, doing yoga, meditating, and exercising, not merely because they're good for my health but because they let me hone my self-awareness skills, which I can then apply minute-to-minute when trying to live out the Nick's culture. These practices also give me a broader, spiritual perspective on my life and our culture. Daily meditation might be part of your morning jog, or you might do it as you wash the dishes in the kitchen. The point is to decide on a "practice" and stay disciplined, even when part of your discipline is to take a week off for a family vacation. The entrepreneur's life is an extreme roller-coaster ride, and so is being a parent. I can't find words to describe the incredible space and peace that my daily spiritual practices have offered me.

Talk about spirituality might seem strange coming from a blue-collar guy. My dad certainly thinks so, and he doesn't hesitate to let me know. When I talk about yoga or meditation, he shakes his head and says, "Are you really going fucking nuts? What the hell is this? I think you better stop making all those trips to California." As I tell him, spirituality and a working-class background are hardly incompatible. The psychologist and educator George Leonard once explained to me that we don't have to be mystics or gods or monks to make a difference in today's world. Today's mystics are all around us, and they look like average men or women doing everyday work that touches people and brings about extraordinary results. As leaders, our job is to integrate mindfulness into our daily lives, in any number of forms, so that we can not only live our company's culture but serve as beacons for others. Working hard and staying focused, we pursue what Buddhism calls the layperson's or "householder's" journey.

INNOVATING YOUR CULTURE

Even as leaders work to embody the culture as it exists in its present state, they must also update and adapt the culture so it stays fresh. This means taking risks and exposing themselves to new ideas, tools, and practices—becoming "comfortable with being uncomfortable." I remember how uncomfortable I felt when I first went to Esalen. I had never been to California before, nor had I spent much time exploring my emotions. As I drove up the magnificent coast on Highway 1, I wasn't thinking about peace and love; I was thinking, "Wow, this place is amazing and beautiful. I need to get my Harley and the guys I ride with up here for a trip." Upon arrival, I found I had to share my two-bedroom cabin with a total stranger, and that I had to participate in a workshop with a couple of dozen other strangers. Believe me, I would have rather been standing in a dark Chicago alley face-to-face with a big, burly guy who wanted to kick my butt—at least that was something I thought I was prepared for.

Over the next few days, I moved past my fears and let my guard down. I learned about spiritual discipline as well as some of the particulars: yoga movements, Aikido warm-ups, the practice of daily personal affirmations, methods of meditation. I wound up returning to Esalen four times over the next three years, and I incorporated elements of what I'd learned into our culture at Nick's. We did and still do physical movements and meditation for forty-five minutes before our weekly manager meetings, inviting everyone in the company to attend. Yes, if you walk by the closed glass doors on a Wednesday afternoon in either one of our restaurants, you will see a group of people on yoga mats. My dad thinks it's silly, but the spiritual practice makes great business sense, allowing us to work together much more efficiently. To some of our managers, it feels like we accomplish four hours of work in a single hour; in effect, we've slowed down, giving ourselves a wonderful reprieve from the normal hectic pace, so that we can speed up.

Esalen was just the beginning of a personal journey that has continued to this day and that continues to fuel evolution in our culture. I've already described how my encounter with the Dalai Lama in 2006 led to us develop systems for observing and shaping behavior. At around that time, my business seemed to be coasting along pretty well overall, yet I felt stuck. I had been working with my consultant and coach, Rudy Miick, for several years, and it didn't feel like he and I were seeing eye-to-eye as much about my business. Also, I was having a hard time finding managers who could operate well within our culture; people I'd hired from outside the company just didn't seem to get what we were all about. I attended a workshop in Chicago organized by the philosopher Ken Wilber in which Wilbur's Integral Theory was described and participants were taught how to put it into practice in a business context. Integral Theory is a comprehensive approach for looking at the world that emphasizes connections between disciplines, worldviews, and philosophies. Wilber helped me think more deeply about Nick's, questioning whether every decision I make integrates all parts of my business. This eventually led me to develop a more balanced decision-making process as well as a comprehensive, holistic perspective that built on all the other personal-development work I was doing. I attained a deep understanding of how every action I took had an impact not only on myself, on a personal level, but also on my people, my culture, the community my business was in, and my brand.

At the Wilber seminar, I met a consultant named Christina Barr, who had a master's degree in Integral Theory. We clicked, and I hired her to serve as my personal coach and to help us with our manager problem. We worked together to articulate seven leadership competencies that aligned with our culture: Commitment to Purpose and Values; Pride in the Brand; Passion for Service and Hospitality; Team Building; Effective Communications; Growing the Business and Affecting the Community; and Self-development. Today when our managers go through 401 training, they receive an additional pamphlet that identifies Nick's as a learning organization, defines each of these competencies in depth, and translates the competencies into specific actions we expect on the part of every manager. Christina also helped us develop a new training module, 501, which helps our leaders work on themselves, aligning their personal values with those of our company. As of this writing, 501 is still unfinished, and I'm not sure we'll need it in the years ahead, but our work reflects my commitment to always push our culture to a higher level.

Besides seminars, retreats, and coaching, I read constantly with an eye toward improving our culture. This is another thing my dad doesn't get; when he sees me reading, he says, "What the hell you reading again for; how much smarter do you want to get?" His attitude probably accounts for why I didn't read any books at all throughout my years at school, and why by the time I was thirty-five years old I had probably made it through exactly one. The book that changed everything for me was George Leonard's *Mastery*, which revealed a framework for thinking about and pursuing discipline in life. At Esalen, after I'd read that book, I had plenty of free time and nothing to do, so I browsed around the retreat's bookstore. A guy saw me staring blankly at the shelves and suggested some books by Ken Wilber, including *A Brief History of Everything*. That book rocked me to the core. I was so excited about the ideas I encountered in it that I would call Rudy in the middle of chapters to tell him what I'd just read. I was more like an eight-year-old at his first major league baseball game than a guy in his thirties who'd just finished a book. I had finally learned the value of reading.

I begin pretty much every day with a cup of coffee and at least a half hour of book time. I gobble up any business or self-development book I can find, from Jim Collins's leadership classic *Built to Last* to Howard Schultz's *Pour Your Heart into It* to Eckhart Tolle's *The Power of Now*. A book I'm reading might lead me to add a page to our manager training, or to create a new structure for meetings, or to develop a whole new marketing system for our catering business. Just the other day, I improved our online business with a new Web page based on insights I got while reading Lisa Gansky's book *The Mesh: Why the Future of Business Is Sharing*. I've also incorporated regular reading into our management training and coaching. As part of 301, every one of our teammates reads George Leonard's *Mastery*. After 401, I send our managers four questions each month to answer about their self-development, including a question on reading they've done over the past month. For each of our Operating Partners, I come up with specific reading programs, and we begin by reading two books together, Richard Boyatzis's *Resonant Leadership* and Karl Weick and Kathleen Sutcliffe's *Managing the Unexpected*. At the end of every chapter, we exchange ideas based on questions I've written. It is a great learning experience—for them and for me.

I've already said that you need to define a great culture by first defining a solid purpose, but if you're still working on articulating what your purpose is and outlining the values you want to share with your team, there are some small things you can try now that will at least help put you on the right track. I'd suggest experimenting with Safe Space (see Chapter Four). It's so basic, so essential, and it will put you in a good position to do the important work of defining a purpose, as described in Chapter One. I would also encourage you to begin cultivating mindfulness in your life. Take a baby step, ten minutes of meditation a day. Experiment with a daily practice that works for you. Explore working with a coach. Read *Mastery* or *The Power of Now*; sometimes a book like this is exactly what we need to come to mindfulness with an open heart.

SAFEGUARDING THE CULTURE

As important as mindfulness and inner discipline are, they are merely a foundation for the cultural warrior's main work: making sure the culture doesn't decay. I devote time each week to walking the restaurants, singling out behaviors that exemplify our purpose and values, such as the carry-out host who engages a guest in conversation, or the host who manages to get a lobby full of guests laughing as they wait for their tables, or one team member who coaches another on performance. I also step in whenever appropriate to correct young team members who are behaving in a way that doesn't serve our purpose. Though I put my managers in charge of following team members' progress and coaching them on how to improve, I try to make ample and strategic use of the attention I garner as the owner and founder.

Once, I was sitting in one of our restaurants working at a

booth, and I ordered salad and pizza for lunch. Jackie, our server, had been working at Nick's for only a month, and just a minute or so after she brought me my salad (which had taken her longer than usual to bring) she returned to inform me that my pizza was ready. Did I want the pizza right away or did I want to wait? I told her to wait so that I could finish my salad, but by the time I was finished and my pizza arrived, it was lukewarm. As the head of the company in this situation, I had several options: Do nothing, offer either Performance Feedback or Direct Feedback, or perform a more extensive Feedback Loop. Since I hadn't had much interaction with Jackie and hadn't built up the necessary rapport, I knew that Direct Feedback and Performance Feedback wouldn't work. Still, I didn't want to just let Jackie's poor performance slide, because that would signal to her that her low performance was acceptable. I wound up spending five minutes on a Feedback Loop with her once the lunch rush had finished and asked ask her to tell me one thing she did well and one thing she could do to enhance her performance. When she didn't bring up her lateness with the salad, I brought it to her attention and led her, through a series of questions, to understand how it screwed up the dining experience for our guests. She was grateful for the coaching and cheerfully assured me that she'd learn from the experience.

Although chance interventions like this with novice teammates can prove very powerful, I make a far bigger impact by coaching our managers and trainers on their coaching of others. One Saturday night at around ten, I stopped in at our Crystal Lake restaurant and found our team working through our standard closing routines. I was walking around, greeting everyone within five steps, smiling, offering words of encouragement, when I saw our manager Scott speaking with our server Maura.

Maura had just begun her 301 training, and my Safe Space radar was on fire. Rather than intervene and micromanage their conversation, I simply said hello and told Scott I would be around the dining room when he was finished talking so we could check in. Five minutes later, when Scott came by, I asked, "Safe Space conversation?" He nodded, and I gave him the thumbs-up. By recognizing his behavior in this way and then moving on to another topic, I affirmed his decision to spend time with Maura as well as my trust in him to get the conversation right without my input.

I also realized that trust alone wasn't enough. Maura had just begun her training as a coach, and I needed to track how well Scott was supporting and coaching her. Two days later, I ran into Maura toward the end of her shift. "Maura, I noticed you and Scott talking on Saturday night in the banquet room. Were you working through a Safe Space issue?"

She said they were.

"Did you get what you needed, and do you feel supported?"

She nodded. "Yeah. Everything's fine." But she seemed tense; her shoulders were bunched up, her hand movements jerky, and her breathing shallow.

"Great," I said. "I don't need all the details, but I would like to hear the take-away from Scott's coaching. What can you improve on in your performance? What will you do differently in the future?"

Maura thought for a moment. "We had a Safe Space because I got upset watching another server do something pretty suspicious. She took a beer off of the tab, and then when the bartender wasn't looking, she poured it herself and served it to the guest. I thought she was stealing, and I thought this was horribly wrong, but I didn't say anything. She has worked here forever, and I felt pretty intimidated. From talking with Scott, I learned that next time I need to step up to the plate and confront her or anyone else I see doing something out of line."

Her use of the word "wrong" triggered alarm bells for me. She was rushing to a definitive judgment about the server, not taking time to explore what was actually known about the situation and consider if her interpretation of the facts was correct.

"Okay," I said, nodding, "and Scott showed you what steps to take when confronting the server in a situation like that?"

She shrugged. "Not really. I just know I need to speak up."

I motioned for her to step aside into a corner where we could speak privately. "Let's replay the tape," I said. "Pretend I'm the server. Tell me what you'd say if you were stepping into the conflict. Just stick to the data."

"Okay. I'd say, 'Nick, I noticed that you just deleted that beer from the bill, and that you then went behind the bar to pour it yourself, without waiting for the bartender to come back. That's wrong, you can't just delete a beer. That's stealing.'"

Pretending I was the server, I said, "Is it wrong? I just want to give these guests a beer on the house."

Maura looked off in the distance, and then shot me a frustrated look. "I just don't know what to do next. All I want to do is tell you how wrong you are."

"But do you really *know* it's wrong?"

"I guess I don't know if it's wrong." She thought about it a moment. "But I do know that it will make our beverage cost off."

"There you go," I said, "that's data. Good job."

I could see the lightbulb go on for her. "Okay, you mean I just need to stick to the facts and have a direct conversation with her instead of accusing her outright."

I nodded. "Absolutely. 'Right' or 'wrong' will take care of

itself. And if you get any resistance from this server, and you start to feel overwhelmed, simply say that you would like to get a third person in on the conversation."

Maura flashed a big smile. Her shoulders relaxed, and her breath moved from her chest to her stomach. "Thanks, Nick. I really appreciate your support."

She moved to get up, but I motioned her to stay. "Wait, Maura. You know part of my work is to teach and coach Scott, right? So I'm curious—what is different, if anything, from how I just coached you as opposed to how Scott coached you on Saturday?"

"Easy," she said. "Today was much more helpful. You walked me through some of the 'how,' which I needed, because I'm still learning how to be a good coach. Scott just told me what I needed to do, but he didn't tell me how. In fact, he kind of brushed me off, suggesting that I should figure it out myself."

"Thanks, Maura. That's very helpful."

I got up and went to find Scott. He was downstairs in our office, doing Feedback Loops with new trainees. As I walked in, he was speaking to a teenaged new-hire and was spot-on in recognizing her positive behaviors. When the new hire left, I made sure to acknowledge him first for engaging well with her. Then I recounted the conversation Maura and I had just had. Rather than react defensively, Scott nodded and said, "You know, Nick, this is great feedback. I forgot how difficult it is for us when we're fresh out of 301 and we have all this new stuff we're tracking and trying to use. I really like how you supported Maura and helped her discover what to do in initiating a conversation. And I hadn't thought about letting her know that she could ask for a third person to support her. I will pay closer attention to those nuances in the future."

All told, I spent about ten to fifteen minutes of my time coaching Maura that night, and another ten or fifteen coaching Scott. Not a huge investment, but think about what would have happened if I hadn't intervened. Scott would have continued to provide sub-par coaching to our emerging trainers and managers, who in turn would have transmitted incomplete knowledge and expertise to our team members. Our culture would have been that much looser and less defined, and our people that much more disillusioned and unhappy. Plus, the relationship between Maura and Scott might have soured, creating unnecessary drama that could easily infect the rest of the team. Over time, these small breakdowns would have snowballed, leading our company down the path to mediocrity. A simple and thoughtful intervention at the managerial level allowed me to not only avoid this outcome, but to build trust between Maura, Scott, and myself. This is the critical daily work of the cultural warrior.

Making it a priority to keep our managers and trainers on track holds an additional benefit: People now come to *me* seeking advice about culturally significant issues. One Sunday afternoon, I was strolling around downtown Chicago when I got a call from Kelsey, our training coordinator, and Nancy, our head of human resources, about another situation that had emerged concerning Scott. After leading our two-day orientation, the two had dismissed a seventeen-year-old kid Scott had hired. The kid had seemed uninvolved, unengaged, and lackluster; he sat slumped in his chair with his arms folded, rolled his eyes, and spoke up only when called upon. Kelsey and Nancy had questioned him about this after the first day and offered him an opportunity to shift his behavior, but he had not. This was the first time in years that anyone had been terminated so soon after being hired.

Nancy and Kelsey wanted to sit down with Scott to let him know that his hire had flopped. I agreed this was a good idea and offered some thoughts about how to proceed. Just two days earlier, I had walked by Scott and Nancy as they were conducting an interview, and saw them give each other a high five in front of the candidate. Although we like to have fun at Nick's, this behavior seemed obviously inappropriate—first, because it was too casual and, second, because it created an insider-outsider dynamic, separating Nancy and Scott from the interviewee. Now, given what had happened in orientation, I advised Nancy to consider whether we had unearthed a pattern in Scott's interviewing behavior that required coaching. Kelsey and Nancy knew roughly how to apply purpose and values in this specific situation, but they hadn't been tracking the potential pattern in Scott's behavior, and so my role here was to go one layer deeper than they did.

In addition to correcting behaviors, I'm also always looking to correct systems that run afoul of our culture. We find it challenging to staff our restaurants so that we have enough people on hand to serve the numbers of guests coming in, but not so many that team members are standing around without work to do. It's a delicate balance, and to sustain it my former Operating Partner, Barry, and our controller, Matt, came up with a complex labor grid that mapped labor against forecasted sales for the day. Using this grid, our scheduling team could assign the right number of team members to work shifts in our Heart of House and Front of House. I kept getting complaints that this system was too complicated and that, as a result, too many or too few people were being called in to work. With the wrong number of people on hand, our guest experience suffered. We were diluting our culture of community service and high performance.

Looking at some of the software we had on hand, I found a way to integrate our labor-assignment process with our time-clock software. The system I created was much more specific to unique parts of the day (that is, the lunch and dinner times) and our hourly sales for each work group. As a result, we were able to become much more accurate in our staffing, not only because our scheduling team was less confused, but because they could understand our needs more precisely. Playing the role of cultural warrior, I steered us away from behavior that ran counter to our culture and toward behavior that supported it.

Another instance in which I helped change systems that eroded our culture has to do with how our managers delegate tasks. For a period of time, Barry and my all-star consultant, Rudy Miick, were complaining that our managers weren't doing enough to get their teams to complete projects we wanted done on time. "They need to step up more," they said.

This complaint of theirs seemed misplaced to me. Our managers were working plenty hard already; they just didn't have enough delegating skills to know how to get more projects out through their teams. They seemed like hamsters in a wheel, spinning it faster but going nowhere, and dragging down our performance in the process. Barry and Rudy's approach would have made it worse, making slave drivers of the managers in our company and sending us back into command-and-control mode.

To help train managers in effective methods of delegating, I reviewed our old system and compared it with what I had recently learned from my friend and wise old retired CFO Deben Tobias. Identifying gaps in our system, I devised an "art" and "science" system for effective delegation and meeting operational commitments. This system became part of our formal 400-level manager training. The results have been great. Projects are getting done on time, and even when circumstances prevent projects from meeting their deadlines, we're aware of that in advance and are able to put contingency plans in place. With more clarity around expectations at the executive level, managers—the people in an organization who usually get squeezed the most—are less stressed, happier, and better able to perform. Here is a situation where the cultural warrior's work has paid immediate and obvious dividends.

SAFEGUARDING THE FINANCES

It's not enough to safeguard the culture. Cultural warriors also have to safeguard the dollars and cents that *underlie* the culture. After all, if the business fails, the culture will cease to exist no matter how much effort you put into it. In particular, I have a responsibility to make sure that both our fiscal reporting processes and the finances underpinning our operations are sound, and that we have a workable strategy in place, complete with contingency plans, for achieving sales, revenue, and profit goals on both a unit and a company-wide basis. For a small business, cultural warriors must assess whether growth is possible and desirable, and if it is, they must steer the company responsibly down that path.

Looking back on it, I performed some parts of the cultural warrior's financial role pretty well. Although I wish I had consulted our balance sheet more closely at the outset, my intention to grow the company and the initial steps we took to support that move did rest on solid ground. To expand responsibly, leaders must have a clear vision and commit themselves wholeheartedly to realizing that vision. My decision to grow Nick's flowed directly from a deep passion I felt. I wanted to share both our pizza and our culture of trust, community, and learning. I wanted to influence other businesses to treat their team members better, showing the world that even minimum-wage service jobs can be fulfilling and meaningful if structured thoughtfully and humanely. I also hoped to see our marketing practices spread so that more schools and community organizations could benefit. Our culture seemed to represent an organic, natural, multilevel way to support communities, and I wanted to put that to the test in Chicago and other low-income urban areas.

Once we decided to grow, I again acquitted myself well as a cultural warrior by setting us up to generate strong sales. When most restaurants open, they hire 50% more staff than they need, assuming that many hires will quit after a month or two. When we opened our Elgin location in 2004, we hired 100 team members, exactly as many as we needed to open our restaurant, and spent a full twenty-eight days training them, including thirty hours dedicated to our culture. This cost us about $80,000, but it was well worth it: When we opened our 350-seat restaurant, our trained team could offer guests the same high-quality experience as a restaurant that had been open for six months. Our sales kicked off at $60,000 per week and stayed at that level, and we lost only five team members during the first six months.

Unfortunately, as I've subsequently learned, sales and revenue aren't everything. All the sales in the world won't save you if your capital structure is unstable. And that's where my performance in the fiscal dimensions of the cultural warrior's role has fallen short—with the balance sheet. It's embarrassing to admit, but for all the time I spent thinking about culture, I spent very little time analyzing how our assets stacked up against our liabilities. Of course, if anyone had asked me if I understood the financials, I would have nodded my head. But I really didn't understand the connections between the different numbers, in part because I didn't obtain adequate advice and coaching.

My CPA had always seen the balance sheet as a stagnant report, a snapshot of the business that to me was not very useful. When I finally involved a CFO, he helped me relate my current assets to my current liability and to understand the impact of that relationship on profits and net cash flow. He had us put together a net operating-profit summary that tracked back over the previous three years and included unit sales for each location. We also started forecasting cash flow weekly and projected the current cash-flow model into the rest of the year.

Beyond involving advisers with real financial know-how, cultural warriors must have access to a financial adviser who is capable of thinking against the grain. One drawback of a culture like ours is its tendency to generate too *much* love, admiration, and positive thinking at times, and our financial team suffered from that. I needed a strategic financial adviser who hadn't drunk the Kool-Aid and whose job it was to inject a little bit of healthy pessimism into the mix. My dad had performed that function well for us, but not in terms of the intricacies of our balance sheet. The result: a strategy for growth that was too rosy, that didn't have adequate contingency plans in place should reality not match our projections, and that therefore put in jeopardy the culture we had labored so diligently to build.

As it turned out, our poor planning led to a major crisis in 2007, which in turn sowed the seeds of the even larger 2011 crisis described in part at the beginning of this book. We had opened a second location in Elgin with the idea of ultimately expanding to five restaurants, each with the same 9,000-square-foot, 350-seat layout as our original location in Crystal Lake. By 2007, with sales climbing steadily at both restaurants, I happened on a promising location on Chicago's northwest side, not exactly my old neighborhood, but very close and one I knew well as a kid (I grew up just a couple of miles away from Wrigley Field). This site afforded us three times the population density of each of our other two restaurants, making for a great business opportunity. I was also excited by the positive impact our culture would have on this inner-city community, especially with our fund-raiser program and our training and development of young adults.

Lacking the capital to purchase this property outright, as I had done before, I worked with the owner, Frank, to negotiate a lease. Although he was a good guy, I sensed a lack of experience, and it took a long time to execute the deal. Still, the lease was advantageous to us, and I found a local lender, LaSalle Bank, that was willing to finance the project. This restaurant would be smaller than the others—only 8,000 square feet and 250 seats— and we'd have smaller property-maintenance costs than at a large suburban location, so I thought our sales per square foot would look better than at our existing locations.

It took a whole year, but by 2008 Frank completed our lease and we were just waiting for approval of our bank loan. We got to work renovating the old building that would be our new home and started hiring and training managers and snapping up the authentic antique materials we needed for the interior. That's when the rumors started that Bank of America was acquiring LaSalle Bank. I asked my neighborhood banker at LaSalle if our deal would still go through. "Yes, of course," he said. "The changeover will be seamless and transparent. Only the banner sign outside our building will change; the rest will stay the same. There's no need for you to seek new financing."

What happened over the next four or five months is a prime

example of what causes many Americans to dislike big corpora-
tions. I had a line of credit out from our other bank, and I kept
drawing down on that, thinking I was going to be reimbursed
when the construction loan was approved. Then Bank of America said they needed more documents. When I got them, they
said they needed more cash down as collateral. I got that as well.
Then in 2008 they wanted me to come up with 50% of the whole
project. Impossible, I told them, I just don't have that kind of
money. At this point, they informed me that they didn't want to
do the project, and that, actually, they didn't do restaurant loans.

I was stunned, distraught, and heartbroken all at once. I
remember hanging up the phone, putting my head down on the
desk, and feeling like I was going to cry. For a week, I thought I
could go to another bank and start over. Then I realized that was
crazy. The economy was already taking a dive, and our Elgin
restaurant was posting the first-ever downward sales trend in
company history. Because I'd abdicated a portion of the cultural
warrior's financial role, we just hadn't planned for a situation
like this; we'd assumed that Elgin's suburban population would
continue to rise, fueled by a boom in housing. Boy, had we been
wrong. We had invested more than $300,000 in the Chicago
site, owed the bank another $200,000, and had no clear plan for
managing that debt. Our very existence was at stake, even
though our guests loved us and we were superstars at generating
sales compared with our peers.

My partner Barry and I decided in September 2008 to hold
off on building a third restaurant. Before finalizing the decision,
we wanted to obtain a consensus from our team, so we called a
company-wide meeting. At that meeting, I let everything out—
both my emotions and the facts about our predicament, including the possibility that we could lose the company. Our team

responded in the best possible way: by sticking together. Our trainers and managers agreed we should abandon our expansion plans and refocus on the existing restaurants. That meant kissing the $300,000 good-bye. We'd have to tighten our bootstraps so our existing restaurants could help us recover the monumental debt we had incurred. By a unanimous vote, the trainers decided to contribute all their profit sharing back to the company until we paid back the debt. I joined them in the sacrifice, taking a 20% pay cut and trading in my Mercedes for a Toyota Prius.

We cobbled together a strategy and a budget that would allow us to discharge our debt within a year. Each restaurant would contribute $700 a day over that period—what Jim Collins would call a BHAG (big hairy audacious goal). Such goals are great, but ours didn't take into account the worsening economy of 2008 and 2009, which made it extremely difficult to generate sales growth, and which necessitated further improvisation on our part in the form of the innovative sales promotions described in previous chapters. Those succeeded for us, but we might have been in a far better place if, in my capacity as cultural warrior, I had put financial benchmarks in place that, once reached, triggered alternate action plans.

If I had thought through the strategy more deeply with financial considerations in mind, we might also have hired people with different forms of expertise to execute our backup plans. Heck, we might have revisited our purpose. Instead, we found ourselves forced to behave reactively. We came up with a series of short-term, marketing-based, Band-Aid solutions rather than true, long-term cures. That's never a good place for a business to be, and it would leave us struggling for our life under a mountain of debt by 2011. The culture we had worked so hard to build—and that I had sworn to protect—was in danger of extinction.

Does culture ultimately pale in importance compared with business basics? Did I render myself vulnerable by spending too much time on culture and not enough on the "fundamentals"? For all my idealism, had I created a business that couldn't, in the end, survive? Was my dad right after all? It took a couple of years and some seriously scary moments, but I finally found out the answers.

TRIUMPH OF THE CULTURE WARRIOR

In March 2011, after returning from a business trip to Florida, I discovered an $87,000 mistake in our cash-flow statement. All of sudden, we had a $50,000 shortfall. We thought we could make up the difference with a new sales initiative, but then we got hit by another whammy: Thanks to a historically rough winter and the bad economy, our new marketing plan had fallen short of forecasted sales over the previous two months. Now all of sudden we were going to fall not $50,000 but about $200,000 short of cash.

I scrambled for help, realizing I needed to go beyond my usual mentors and coaches. A friend put me in touch with a hard-edged, veteran finance guy from New York. Reviewing our balance sheet, he minced no words: Our financial situation was way out of whack. Thanks to a bad real estate deal we'd put together for our second restaurant (and the third that failed to materialize), our capital structure was messed up, and we had way more debt than our two wildly successful restaurants could handle. We were losing $30,000 each month; even if we increased sales by 300%, we could never make up the ground we needed to cover in order to pay our interest charges. If we couldn't get the banks to refinance, I would lose my business.

As I sat there on the phone in a busy coffee shop, my body went numb. The world seemed to fall away. Every word I heard seemed deafening, penetrating every cell of my body. At the same time, I felt unwavering gratitude that I was now learning a truth about my business, and that I still had a chance to turn things around. I went straight to work with my CPA and financial adviser Gerry to devise an action plan. We would approach the bank for new financing and in the meantime take steps to reduce overhead to the bare minimum while building up sales as much as possible. If we could stay current with our investors until October, we would probably be in good shape. A new Walmart was scheduled to open up that month across the street from our Elgin location, and we hoped this would lead to increased traffic past the restaurant and a sizable bump in sales. With a reduced debt load, we would then be able to attract new investment into our company or, failing that, stick it out ourselves through increased sales.

As Gerry and I spoke, I remembered a time as a kid when I had been on the losing side of a fight. The kid who took me down asked if I gave up; when I replied no, he laid into me with more punches. He may have gotten the best of me, but he came away with a black eye, too. He would always remember me and wouldn't want to mess with me again. I learned that if I didn't quit, if I could deal with a little pain, I could get through anything.

This time, I was in for more than just a little pain. Approaching my investors was a humbling experience, as I had to admit I had screwed up and beg them to forgive the balance of what I owed them in exchange for a piece of Nick's. Although most investors seemed sympathetic, a few lectured me about all I had done wrong, saying I needed to spend more time in the restaurants and cut benefits for our team members. In the meantime, sales actually *declined* by about 30% through the spring and summer, thanks to road construction outside our Elgin location. We responded with all kinds of creative sales initiatives, including an "end of construction" party on Labor Day weekend, but these at best brought only minor and temporary sales upticks. We managed to make money in June, but in July we were in the red again, and slim profits in August and September did not ease our cash-flow problems. Meanwhile, we were also doing everything possible to trim overhead, including cutting salaries, negotiating longer terms with our vendors, letting one salaried manager go, and accepting the offers of some team members to take unpaid time off. I myself went without a paycheck for ninety days.

Our bank so far wouldn't agree to restructure our loans. In July the New York financial expert suggested we force our bank's hand by threatening to go into a restructuring bankruptcy. He said I'd need "balls of steel" and warned me not to back down with the bank, even if this meant purposely missing a couple of mortgage payments. Following his advice, I hired a bankruptcy attorney, but the bank wouldn't budge. Claiming their hands were tied, bank management suggested I sell the Elgin location to an investment group and solve my problem by negotiating an affordable rent. Unfortunately, that wasn't an option: Real estate values had declined so much that selling the property would have allowed me to pay off only half of what I owed the bank.

I seemed to be facing a brick wall, and it was taking a physical toll. I had been working crazy hours at the restaurant while also meeting with bank officials, lawyers, and investors.

Although I was still exercising regularly, I had stopped doing my yoga practice and wasn't getting enough sleep. On Labor Day weekend, I attended a wedding and afterward suffered excruciating back pains. I was diagnosed with herniated discs and had to spend the next ten days in bed, heavily medicated. When I finally resurfaced, I looked at our cash flows and found the business in dire straits. Our sales forecasts weren't coming close; our revenues were short by a couple of thousand dollars each day. I had hoped we would find ourselves in a decent position by October, but in fact we faced huge red ink. In a couple of weeks, we wouldn't even be able to make our payroll, not to mention pay some of our bills and mortgages.

I spent the next week going over the numbers again and again, trying to figure out what else we could do. I talked to Gerry and Rudy and my Operating Partners. Finally, toward the end of September, I found myself at that moment of desperation described at the beginning of this book. Throwing up my hands, I wrote a hugely risky e-mail in which I admitted my shortcomings and asked the community to come to our rescue. Reprinted below is the full e-mail, the one I wound up sending to 16,000 people on our bulk e-mail list despite the objections of our public relations firm:

> I have never understood why owners or management of a failing company usually don't give others close to the company—especially customers—fair warning about what is going on. In many instances, the team, the core family that built the business, has showed up to work and found the doors locked. I have always said I would never do that to the people I truly care about and owe my life to.

I realize that posting something like this is risky and unorthodox, but I don't care because I don't have anything to fear or hide. We run our business with totally open books, and the core team that shows up at our weekly fiscal huddles will not be surprised by what I'm writing. I truly care about our team and each guest who has blessed us by choosing to eat at Nick's instead of any of the many other places available to them.

As of the beginning of this last week, the hard reality facing us has become glaringly apparent to me. We overbuilt and overspent, and then we didn't cut fast enough or hard enough when sales started to go downhill. The issue is primarily with our Elgin restaurant, but because we are one company, the failure of Elgin will likely impact Crystal Lake as well, depending on the choices our bank makes. This failure is not the fault of our team members; on the contrary, I am extremely grateful to them for their incredible contributions, including accepting salary cuts, taking on more responsibilities, and volunteering to market us on their own time. The whole responsibility for our troubles is mine, for making the bad decisions that got us into this mess.

I realize that many of you out there see a busy restaurant and don't understand how we cannot be profitable or, as many of you have expressed, how we could not be "rolling in cash." We do bring in a lot of revenue, but unfortunately that is not enough to cover our mortgages and the other expenses that accrue from having such large facilities. In 2008, sales at our Elgin location began to drop, causing that location to lose money.

Fortunately, Crystal Lake was profitable enough to cover both restaurants most of the time. As of this year, that's no longer true. The sales drop in Elgin alone has been 30% since last year and close to 50% since 2007, thanks largely to the bad economy and road construction.

We thought that the opening of a new Walmart across the street from Elgin on October 26 would bring enough new traffic to save that location and our company. Unfortunately, the bills that we have been pushing back this year are catching up with us now, about four weeks short of the finish line. Barring some sort of miracle, we are going to run out of cash to pay our vendors and team members over the next couple of weeks and will have to close. Believe me, I have already tried everything possible and would not be writing this if the amount we needed was not many thousands of dollars more than I personally could come up with. I really did believe we were going to make it to the finish line and pull through this, but I have nothing left that I can sell, pawn, or promise—just my business, which now is on the table.

I do have one last hope for me and the 200 team members of Nick's. If within these next four weeks we could see a large increase in sales at either of our restaurants, we could still pull through. SO MY FINAL REQUEST IS FOR EACH OF YOU TO COME TO NICK'S NOW AND TELL AS MANY PEOPLE AS POSSIBLE TO COME NOW! Even if you don't wish to see us survive and continue to be a part of the community, then at least come to say good-bye. If you wish to contact me with investor ideas or any ideas or questions at all, you can e-mail me at office@nickspizzapub .com, call me at 815-356-5557, or simply stop by and talk in person.

Thank you—Nick Sarillo

So, did the community we'd worked so hard and so transparently to serve come to our aid? Yes, it did—beyond my wildest dreams! Within five minutes, several people called the restaurant to order pizza. Within fifteen minutes, a company called to book a banquet with us, and individuals began to arrive telling us they had come to support us. After twenty minutes, my e-mail was posted all over Facebook, and later that day a "Save Nick's" Facebook page popped up as well as a "Pizzapolooza" Facebook event. By 5:30 that afternoon, my bank representative called and left a message saying that the bank had heard about my e-mail from board members and staff, and that they were receiving many requests to help us through this crisis.

Over the next week, we received hundreds of letters of support, including offers of investment money and help from accountants, marketers, and other business professionals. Most critically, we saw a *doubling* of our sales—an increase of $50,000! Our restaurants were jam-packed from open to close; guests happily waited two hours for a table, and some even offered to pay more than the normal price of their food. Tipped off by one of our guests, the media took notice. NBC News and Fox News ran national stories about my e-mail and the response, and they were joined by several local newspapers and pizza-industry publications. By my PR firm's estimate, the PR value alone generated by my e-mail ran into the hundreds of thousands of dollars.

Sales dropped soon after the first week, although they stayed up to 80% above normal for four subsequent weeks, allowing us to make our payroll and get current with our vendors. Afterward, as sales stabilized at about 5% to 10% higher than pre-crisis levels, I approached the bank again to request a loan modification. This time, I came armed with a new business plan that offered projections out to 2015. I had created this plan with the help of Jim, a local accountant who had seen the news of our impending demise and volunteered to help free of charge. In December 2011, with Jim negotiating by my side, the bank finally agreed to forgive payments of the principal on our loan for close to a full year. This would cut our mortgage payments in half, bringing our occupancy percentage (rent and taxes as a percentage of revenues) down to 8% from where it had been before—16% to 18%. The bank also agreed to ask the Small Business Administration to forgive my payments over the same period. We would have the time we needed to stabilize our business. Our crisis was over! To top off that outstanding news, I learned that Nick's had won a "Love Your Local Business" contest sponsored by Intuit, with prize money worth $25,000.

As of this writing, sales remain strong and our financial picture under Jim's business plan looks brighter. I owe all this to our community, which pulled together and decided that the culture we had built was worth saving. My own incompetence in failing to understand the cultural warrior's financial duties had brought us to the brink, but our culture, which had always been bigger than me, pulled us through. If we had been just another restaurant, I seriously doubt the community would have done what it did, and you would instead see a FOR RENT sign on our doors today, just as you do on so many commercial properties across the country. Sustaining culture requires financial acuity and responsibility on the part of leaders, but culture has a financial value as well. It may not be fully quantifiable, but take it from me—that value appears in spectacular form just when you need it most.

STAYING INSPIRED

With our financial crisis now behind us, I'm confident we'll learn from our mistakes and do better in the future. I'm more positive, determined, and happier than ever. This leads me to the fifth and final dimension of the cultural warrior's role: staying inspired at all times, so that everyone else feels motivated to push the culture ever higher. People work for a company like mine because they seek meaningful work. They want to be inspired—by the company and by its leader. As a cultural warrior, I have an obligation to stay positive and energized even in the darkest of days. If I don't continue to believe in the company, then who will?

We all have our own ways of staying positive and avoiding depression in the face of adversity. We can attend religious services, look inward via meditation, take time out to clear our heads, turn to family and friends for reassurance. I do all of these, but I find that the most effective way of inspiring myself is to simply observe the good things happening in our business and the impact it is having on the community.

When our financial crisis broke out and I investigated selling our Elgin location, I spoke to two restaurant real estate specialists, each of whom reviewed our operations inside and out and told me the same thing: They could sell my restaurant and make a big commission for us, but they didn't want to do that. Instead, they would forgo the commission and help me avoid a sale, because they believed in what we did for the community. "Nick," the first guy told me, "I told my wife that I was working with you and the situation you were in, and she said I have to help you through this, because we love Nick's and we don't want it to be anything else." The next real estate guy said, "Nick, I have been coming here with my family for years [he lived about forty-five minutes away from Elgin]. You are doing amazing things here, and this will be a great location. I will go to the bank with you at no charge and share with them why Nick's makes sense at this location." He did go to the bank and spent hours working with my banker. This made a big impression: The banker shared his intention to support us as much as he could and figure out a way to help us restructure our loans.

I also talked to the Small Business Administration (SBA) to learn about our options if higher, pre-recession sales didn't return soon. The SBA guy called me on a Saturday and said he would come out later that day to take pictures of the Elgin location and discuss my situation with me. "I come there with my wife and sons all the time," he said. "You are doing all the right things. We need to help you get through this. I know this area well, and you just need to bridge this gap. We will get you there; my wife would kill me if she knew I could help you and didn't do everything possible."

Reactions like this in times of crisis affirm for me that despite any shortcomings on my part, we've built something special at Nick's. Something real. Something that can and will endure. Culture alone cannot make a business, but it will sustain you through the rough spots. And the mere knowledge that we've made a difference gives me the strength I need to get up another day and fight the good fight, even when the odds seem overwhelming.

The emotional responses we received to my last-ditch e-mail will stay with me forever. As the guests flowed in with their families and friends and asked to be seated with their favorite servers and bartenders, they also shared with us what Nick's meant to them. In the middle of one busy dinner shift, I walked up to Maura, the server in Crystal Lake, and noticed she was crying. "Nick, go up to table 81 and listen to the little boy sitting with his father tell you how important Nick's is to him and his dad. You will be crying too." On another occasion, a woman in her seventies pulled me aside and reminded me that she had known me many years earlier, when as a high school senior I had dated her neighbor's daughter. "Have you ever seen the movie *It's a Wonderful Life*?" she asked me with tears in her eyes. "Nick, this is just like that movie. You are just like the character George Bailey. Look how the community is turning out to support you. I am so proud of what you have accomplished." Before she would let me go, she gave me a big hug.

Similar boosts of support popped up on Facebook and via e-mail. Guests applauded my e-mail's honesty and communicated how much our restaurants have meant to them and to our community over the years. As one guest e-mailed, "I love Nick's and have always felt I made friends with your staff. . . . I had my son's first birthday party in your back room, and my husband and I have always said that was the BEST birthday party we ever had. Nick, you really seem like you care about everyone, and I am amazed at your honesty. This has to be so hard." Another posted on Facebook: "We have so many fond family memories of Nick's Pizza. Nick's has been such a generous contributor to our communities in the form of fund-raising. We will be ordering some pizza for sure!" And a third wrote: "I think everyone in the area needs to band together and order/dine in 10x more than normal in the coming weeks to do whatever we can to save this location. Hoping for a miracle and promoting the heck out of your business as I always do!" Some individuals writing from out of town even offered to send checks in lieu of eating at our restaurants.

As incredible as it has been, the lift I've received from the community pales against that derived from another source: our team members. In keeping with our ethic of transparency, I told the team within a few weeks about our initial crisis in 2008. Not long thereafter, our manager Amy e-mailed her fellow managers sharing that we had saved $1,200 in a single month by doing away with our policy of free meals for salaried managers. I didn't know what this was all about. The next day, I saw Amy in the office. "Well, yeah," she said, "you weren't a part of the first e-mail that went out, because I didn't copy you. In that e-mail, I asked the team if instead of receiving all our meals for free, we'd pay 50% for our food, just like the rest of the company. The whole team responded immediately, saying, 'Yes, they'd do this in a heartbeat to support the company.' I was as shocked as you were that we saved that much in just one period on food."

I was impressed that the team had stepped up and contributed without me even asking. But I couldn't understand why Amy hadn't copied me on the initial e-mail. If she had, I would have modeled the desired behavior as well by paying for half of my meals.

"We purposely didn't want you to do that," Amy said. "Are you kidding me? You've sacrificed enough already. You gave up your Mercedes. You're always working hard. This is something we wanted to do ourselves for the company and for you."

I was blown away and energized more than ever to do whatever I could to build the company. Our team's show of support hardly ended there. They formed "super sales spectacular SWAT teams," groups of team members who volunteered to go out to businesses within a five-mile radius of our restaurants to pass out menus and flyers. Other team members worked hard to generate sales at school functions and community events. They used Facebook to ask their friends to visit them at work.

In 2011, when we were veering toward bankruptcy, our team members again stepped up. Some volunteered to take unpaid leave, while others who had been working in higher-paid administrative positions volunteered to go back to lower-paid server jobs for the time being. Our team members also inspired me with their professionalism and dedication during an all-team meeting we held in August 2011. It was an especially challenging time. We had already cut overhead in our attempt to make it to October and the Walmart opening, but now, with many local businesses downsizing and the daytime population in Crystal Lake declining, our weekday lunch business was generating only half the revenue required to remain profitable, and we were shutting it down. In support of cutting our overhead cost, we also had to lay off George, our restaurant accountant, and ask Kelsey, our training coordinator, to take a sabbatical from training and return to her earlier role as a server. George had been with us for six years, starting at age sixteen. Going into the meeting, I had wondered whether team members would understand these moves, given that we were still keeping on Jill, a recently hired team member, as our accountant at about the same salary George received, and that we had hired Al, a veteran salesperson, to develop our catering/outside sales.

Thankfully, our culture of openness and Safe Space came through for us. As I went through the rationales for all of these moves, presenting the fiscal data, team members asked some probing questions, but they also realized that the situation we faced required tough decisions. It helped that I announced I would be taking no salary for the next ninety days. In the end, the team emerged from the meeting with its morale intact and, if anything, even stronger. Team members got right to work, sharing sales techniques with one another and brainstorming how individuals could build new sales by mobilizing their personal networks. The day after our all-team meeting, Al, our new sales guy, stunned me by volunteering to work through the end of 2011 with no pay.

"I was so moved by what I saw and heard yesterday from the team," he told me. "I can get by for a little while without getting paid, and I want to do my part to help us get through this."

Can you imagine that? Here was a guy who had just joined our organization, and he too felt inspired to contribute. I felt overwhelmed with gratitude.

It took so many people giving of themselves from the bottom of their hearts and in so many ways to save our business and get through 2011. On the day in September when I sent out the last-ditch e-mail, I had wondered how our team would respond, but almost every team member at our Elgin restaurant announced he or she would work for free that day. Even after all they had already done on our behalf during the previous several months, team members at both restaurants were so moved by the e-mail that they sent it aggressively to family and friends in an attempt to save Nick's.

Cultural warriors ultimately sustain a virtuous circuit of inspiration: Their positive energy raises up the spirits of others, which in turn renews the cultural warrior's dedication, so that he or she can continue to embody, protect, sustain, and develop the culture. Even seemingly insurmountable problems seem more manageable, and companies and cultures have more staying power than they otherwise would have.

This chapter has focused on the leader's unique role in building the "secret ingredient" at Nick's, our high-performance culture. With the systems this book describes in place, it's certainly possible for an effective leader to escape to Florida and leave it to others to push the purpose ahead. Yet there is so much to be gained if leaders take the purpose as seriously as possible and embrace the mantle of cultural warrior. In fact, leaders stand to gain as much as anyone else. Your company's purpose is something you believe in—an extension of your personality—so by definition you'll become happier by working as intensely as possible and at all times to bring it to fruition.

To conclude this book, I'd like to call on all of us to improve not just our companies, but ourselves and the world around us. Every moment is a job interview, for everybody in the company, including *us*. Any action we take in the world becomes an opportunity to affirm our purpose. If we strive to be mindful at all times, to further our cultures with a warrior's strength and determination, we will win, as will those with the good fortune to work for us.

I must share with you one more story. Alejandro is a slight, shy, soft-spoken man, a Mexican immigrant in his midthirties who had worked as a laborer for my brother's construction company. He is poor and has lived a tough life in the United States apart from his family, who still reside in Mexico. Sometimes Alejandro has had to walk to work in bitter cold and snow because he couldn't afford a car. We first hired him in early 2010 on a project basis to clean the baseboards in one of our restaurants. He could barely speak English, yet he would hear and see our team working, and he became curious. This wasn't like other restaurants where he'd worked. People here were, in his words, like a *familia*. They always seemed to be having fun and were very friendly with one another. They seemed to behave like they were at home. They treated each other with respect.

In August 2010, we needed temporary help, so we asked Alejandro if he'd like to wash dishes for a week or two. He did such a great job that we made it permanent. We got him in orientation and he became a team member, certifying in pizza making. He has really enjoyed working and is learning English with the high school kids who are turning to him for help with their Spanish classes. Alejandro's self-confidence is soaring. He became our employee of the month, an honor he had never received before. For the first time, he said, he felt that people were noticing and appreciating his work.

In February 2011, on Super Bowl Sunday, Alejandro attended a company meeting in which I showed a video of a speech delivered by the marketing consultant Simon Sinek. Sinek's message to businesses is that they need to understand not just *what* they do on a day-to-day basis or *how* they go about doing these things, but *why* they do them in the first place. This is exactly what I mean by purpose.

After our session, Alejandro approached me and said, "Nick, how long you do this? The restaurant, I mean. Why you do this thing like you do?"

"Because I love it," I said. "Because of our purpose."

He looked up at me, a big smile on his face. "This place is truly amazing."

"Thanks," I said.

"No, I mean it. You really feel the *cariño* [affection or loving care]."

"Yes," I said, patting him on the back. "You really do."

A NOTE ON THE JACKET

The jacket photograph and all the photographs in this book are the work of Ben Rodig, another one of our star black-hat trainers in the Heart of House. I am grateful to Ben for putting his heart into these works of art and modeling our value of honoring "individual passions, and creativity at work and at home." I was really excited when I learned that our publisher had accepted Ben's jacket photo, because having a team member's work on the jacket reflects everything I write about in this book, and because Ben truly exemplifies what is possible when people choose to build a company around a strong culture.

When Ben first started with us, he was this tall, skinny, shy sixteen-year-old with thick glasses. Not exactly the perfect hire. Over time, Ben has grown more confident in himself. I remember the Friday night when Ben came into Nick's with his first date. It was his night off, he had a new hairstyle, his glasses were gone, and his clothes were stylin'.

As he walked through the restaurant, introducing his date

to everyone as if he were king, I thought to myself, "Shy young Ben is long gone!"

Today I feel proud of Ben as if he were my own son, and I am inspired, for I see future success stories in each new sixteen-year-old we hire.

ACKNOWLEDGMENTS

My deepest gratitude goes out to the whole team at Nick's Pizza & Pub. I have been incredibly fortunate to have worked alongside all of you as we've built this unique company together. Thank you, too, for being so candid in sharing your stories during preparation of this book. A special thank you to our Operating Partners, Scott Jewitt and Jenny Petersen, for their unwavering support and high energy through our many trials and celebrations.

I also applaud the folks at Portfolio: Adrian Zackheim for believing in me, and Brooke Carey for her attention to detail and for just being a total joy to work with. This book would not have been possible without the support of Lorin Rees, my friend and agent. He found me, guided me, and brought together this tremendous A-team. Thank you, Lorin.

A special thank-you to each of my mentors for their artful guidance along this journey toward publication—Sonia Nevis, Mary Ann Kraus, Deborah Adele, Bo Burlingham, Norm Brodsky, and Yogiraj Achala (Charles Bates). I also wish to acknowledge my large debt to mentors who have been there day in and day out for many years: Gerry Adams, Deben Tobias, and Christina Barr.

To Seth Schulman, my friend and partner in writing this book: You are a truly talented man and, in fact, a fellow carpenter. I never thought I would meet anyone more committed to details than I was until I worked with you. Thank you for teaching, coaching, pushing, and most of all inspiring me to create this work. Your drive and passion make you a man clearly in service to his purpose.

And of course, Rudy Miick. He showed up in my life as if by magic and has since been an incredibly positive influence—not merely as a consultant, but as a mentor, partner, and exceptional friend. I am so grateful for having had the opportunity to bring his ideas to life, and even more grateful for his help in my personal development. He has an uncanny ability to know when to push and when to let go. Thank you, Rudy, for your patience— and for your impatience.

With all my heart, I extend love and gratitude to my mom and dad, Sandra and Nick; my sister, Domenica; and my brother, Tony. We have always been there for each other no matter what. I express appreciation to my former wife, Kathleen, and credit her with the beautiful children we have. To my niece, Gina LeBike, and nephews, Dominic Cresap and Anthony Cresap, thank you for your efforts to stay close as a family and for sharing so many laughs with me during our Sunday pasta dinners.

INDEX